my revision notes

~~OVERNIGHT~~

Edexcel A-level
POLITICS
POLITICAL IDEAS

Neil McNaughton

David Tuck

Series Editor:
Eric Magee

HODDER
EDUCATION
AN HACHETTE UK COMPANY

Acknowledgements

David Tuck would like to thank: his wife Valentina and his parents; James Benefield from Hodder Education, Phil Mander of City of London School for Boys, Nick Gallop of Stamford School and Professor Rob Johns of the University of Essex.

Every effort has been made to trace all copyright holders, but if any have been inadvertently overlooked, the Publishers will be pleased to make the necessary arrangements at the first opportunity.

Although every effort has been made to ensure that website addresses are correct at time of going to press, Hodder Education cannot be held responsible for the content of any website mentioned in this book. It is sometimes possible to find a relocated web page by typing the address of the home page for a website in the URL window of your browser.

Hachette UK's policy is to use papers that are natural, renewable and recyclable products and made from wood grown in sustainable forests. The logging and manufacturing processes are expected to conform to the environmental regulations of the country of origin.

Orders: please contact Bookpoint Ltd, 130 Park Drive, Milton Park, Abingdon, Oxon OX14 4SE. Telephone: (44) 01235 827827. Fax: (44) 01235 400401. Email education@ bookpoint.co.uk Lines are open from 9 a.m. to 5 p.m., Monday to Saturday, with a 24-hour message answering service. You can also order through our website: www. hoddereducation.co.uk

ISBN: 978-1-4718-8969-1

First published in 2017 by

Hodder Education,

An Hachette UK Company

Carmelite House

50 Victoria Embankment

London EC4Y 0DZ

www.hoddereducation.co.uk

Impression number   10   9   8   7   6   5   4   3   2

Year   2021   2020   2019   2018

Typeset in Bembo Std 11/13 by Integra Software Services Pvt. Ltd., Pondicherry, India

Printed in India

A catalogue record for this title is available from the British Library.

Get the most from this book

Everyone has to decide his or her own revision strategy, but it is essential to review your work, learn it and test your understanding. These Revision Notes will help you to do that in a planned way, topic by topic. Use this book as the cornerstone of your revision and don't hesitate to write in it – personalise your notes and check your progress by ticking off each section as you revise.

Tick to track your progress

Use the revision planner on page 4 to plan your revision, topic by topic. Tick each box when you have:

- revised and understood a topic
- tested yourself
- practised the exam questions and gone online to check your answers and complete the quick quizzes.

You can also keep track of your revision by ticking off each topic heading in the book. You may find it helpful to add your own notes as you work through each topic.

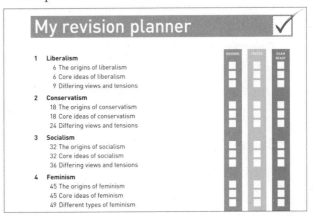

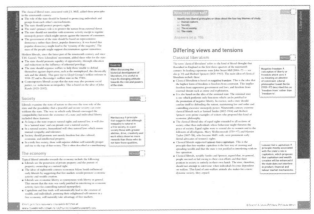

Features to help you succeed

Exam tips and summaries

Expert tips are given throughout the book to help you polish your exam technique in order to maximise your chances in the exam. The summaries provide a quick-check bullet list for each topic.

Typical mistakes

The authors identify the typical mistakes candidates make and explain how you can avoid them.

Now test yourself

These short, knowledge-based questions provide the first step in testing your learning. Answers are at the back of the book.

Key words

Clear, concise definitions of essential key words are provided where they first appear.

Revision activities

These activities will help you to understand each topic in an interactive way.

Online

Go online to check your answers to the exam questions and try out the extra quick quizzes at **www.hoddereducation.co.uk/myrevisionnotes**.

My revision planner

Exam practice answers and quick quizzes at
www.hoddereducation.co.uk/myrevisionnotesdownloads

Countdown to my exams

6–8 weeks to go

- Start by looking at the specification. Make sure you know exactly what material you need to revise and the style of the examination. Use the revision planner on page 4 to familiarise yourself with the topics.
- Organise your notes, making sure you have covered everything on the specification. The revision planner will help you group your notes into topics.
- Work out a realistic revision plan that will allow you time for relaxation. Set aside days and times for all the subjects that you need to study, and stick to your timetable.
- Set yourself sensible targets. Break your revision down into focused sessions of around 40 minutes, divided by breaks. These Revision Notes organise the basic facts into short, memorable sections to make revising easier.

REVISED ☐

4–6 weeks to go

- Read through the relevant sections of this book and refer to the exam tips, typical mistakes and key terms. Tick off the topics as you feel confident about them. Highlight those topics you find difficult and look at them again in detail.
- Test your understanding of each topic by working through the 'Now test yourself' questions in the book. Look up the answers in the Answers section on pages 106–112.
- Make a note of any problem areas as you revise, and ask your teacher to go over these in class.
- Look at past papers. They are one of the best ways to revise and practise your exam skills. Write or prepare planned answers to the questions in the exam checklists in the book. Check your answers online at **www.hoddereducation.co.uk/ myrevisionnotesdownloads**.
- Try different revision methods. For example, you can make notes using mind maps, spider diagrams or flashcards.
- Track your progress using the revision planner and give yourself a reward when you have achieved your target.

REVISED ☐

One week to go

- Try to fit in at least one more timed practice of an entire past paper and seek feedback from your teacher, comparing your work closely with the mark scheme.
- Check the revision planner to make sure you haven't missed out any topics. Brush up on any areas of difficulty by talking them over with a friend or getting help from your teacher.
- Attend any revision classes put on by your teacher. Remember, he or she is an expert at preparing people for examinations.

REVISED ☐

The day before the examination

- Flick through these Revision Notes for useful reminders – for example, the exam tips, typical mistakes and key terms.
- Check the time and place of your examination.
- Make sure you have everything you need – extra pens and pencils, tissues, a watch, bottled water.
- Allow some time to relax and have an early night to ensure you are fresh and alert for the examinations.

REVISED ☐

1 Liberalism

The origins of liberalism

- The origins of liberalism can be traced back to the Reformation, when the authoritarian control of the Catholic Church over philosophical and religious thought was challenged by Protestantism, which proposed free will and individualism. This refers mainly to the sixteenth and seventeenth centuries.
- Then came the Enlightenment period, when the idea of rationalism replaced traditional ideas based on religious doctrine. Rationalism refers to ideas which are scientifically or philosophically determined rather than being the result of emotional or religious responses. This period coincides with the late seventeenth century and the whole eighteenth century.
- The age of revolutions (America and France principally) saw the replacement of traditional monarchy by government by consent and representative democracy.
- The new ideas associated with the rise of market capitalism included the importance of free trade and free markets, free of state control. It was also the age of support for enlightened self-interest governing people's economic actions.

> **Social contract** A very early liberal principle dating back to John Locke. This is the idea that the state is based on a contract between the people and the government. While government agrees to make itself accountable to the people and to operate within the law, the people should agree to obey the laws and uphold the security of the state. The US Constitution is a key practical example of a social contract.

Key thinker

John Locke (1632–1704)

Locke is a key figure as he was one of the first Enlightenment thinkers who applied his thought to the nature of government.

The main ideas of John Locke were as follows:
- The state is not the creation of any spiritual creator, nor is it the possession of a monarch who claimed the 'divine right of kings' to govern. Instead the state has to be the creation of humankind. This was the principle of 'government by consent'.
- Before the state existed, humankind lived in a state of nature. In the state of nature, humankind was subject to natural laws and could claim natural rights.
- The laws should follow and confirm natural rights and natural laws.
- The state was the result of a **social contract** between citizens and the government. Government was subject to the consent of the people, in return for which the people agreed to obey its laws.
- Government should be limited and its powers should be divided between different agencies, largely government and an elected parliament.
- There should be tolerance of alternative religious and political views.

Core ideas of liberalism

Human nature

REVISED

The classical liberal view of human nature included the following:
- Rejecting the conservative and Catholic idea that human nature is flawed and humankind is not capable of improvement, early liberals saw individuals as enlightened and rational and capable of self-improvement.

- John Locke and J.S. Mill both argued that people can use their rationality to achieve good ends for themselves and for society.
- People are able to reach rational conclusions through tolerance, reasoned arguments and philosophical considerations.
- Individualists are naturally self-seeking and likely to pursue their self-interest.
- Though individuals are naturally competitive, they are also sensitive to the interests of others.

The state

REVISED

The liberal attitude to the state, its size, role and limits, is critical to an understanding of the development of liberalism and to the different forms of liberalism that have emerged over three centuries. Study of liberalism and the state, therefore, should be chronological in nature.

The original liberal position concerning the state included the following features:

- As, in a state of nature, there are bound to be conflicts between individuals and groups, the state should exist to reduce conflict.
- The laws established by the state should be based on a liberal conception of natural law — that people should respect each other's life, liberty and property.
- The state should promote tolerance.
- The liberal state should be democratic.
- The state should promote meritocracy, where those with greatest ability can progress (see page 8).
- The state should be organised on the basis of rational ideas of government rather than on traditional principles. Thus constitutional government should replace arbitrary government and traditional monarchy. Government should be based on the principle of **limited government**. The best way of limiting the power of government is to divide power between different branches of government. This is the principle of the **separation of powers** as expounded by French philosopher Baron de Montesquieu (1689–1755).

Typical mistake

It is inaccurate to state that the state is the enemy of liberalism — the opposite is actually true. Liberals believe the state is essential to regulate actions by individuals and groups which do harm to others. Though liberals have an optimistic view of human nature and behaviour, they accept that people will not always choose 'good' actions over harmful actions, so the state must control their behaviour. Liberals also believe that state welfare is needed to defend the interests of those who are unable to guarantee their own welfare.

- The state should be based on the principle of 'government by consent'. In one way or another, the people should have the opportunity to show their consent to be governed. This can be done through constitutional agreements and by government which is constantly accountable to the people.
- The state should operate the rule of law, whereby all citizens would enjoy **foundational equality**.
- The state should tolerate and protect the interests of minorities.

Limited government The principle that governments should be constrained by strong laws and constitutions. Liberals believe strongly in limited government. The opposite of limited government is arbitrary government or authoritarian government. In particular, liberals support entrenched constitutions and the separation of powers to reinforce limited government.

Separation of powers An early liberal idea, associated with Montesquieu, which proposed that the three branches of government — legislature, executive and judiciary — should be separated from each other and should have the ability to control each other's power. This prevents the concentration of power in too few hands.

Foundational equality A fundamental liberal belief that all individuals are born with natural rights which entitle them to liberty, the pursuit of happiness and avoidance of pain. It also entitles them to private property. In a liberal state this translates into the rule of law, where all individuals are treated equally under the law.

The classical liberal state, associated with J.S. Mill, added these principles in the nineteenth century:

- The role of the state should be limited to protecting individuals and groups from each other's encroachments.
- The state should protect property rights.
- The state's primary role is to protect the nation from external threat.
- The state should not interfere with economic activity except to regulate monopoly power which might operate against the interests of consumers.
- The government of the state should be based on representative democracy rather than direct, popular democracy. It was feared that popular democracy might lead to the 'tyranny of the majority'. The mass of the people might support discrimination against minorities.

Modern liberals, since the latter part of the nineteenth century and since T.H. Green's 'New Liberalism' movement, added these roles for the state:

- The state should promote equality of opportunity, through education and reductions in the influence of inherited privilege.
- The state should organise welfare to help those unable to defend themselves against deprivation, such as the unemployed, the chronically sick and the elderly. This gave rise to Lloyd George's welfare reforms in 1918–22 and to Beveridge's welfare state in the 1940s.
- Contemporary liberals accept that the state may also promote social justice, i.e. reductions in inequality. This is based on the ideas of John Rawls (1921–2002).

> **Exam tip**
>
> When discussing the historical development of liberalism, it is useful to trace its changing attitude towards the role and powers of the state.

Society

REVISED

Liberals examine the state of nature to discover the true role of the state and the possibility that a peaceful and secure society can exist without the state. The way in which early liberals envisaged the compatibility between the existence of a state and individual liberty included these features:

- As long as the state respects natural rights and natural law, it will also be a 'natural state' and can preside over a natural society.
- In a natural society, humankind will obey natural laws which ensure mutual sympathy and tolerance.
- Society should promote not merely freedom but also cultural, economic and intellectual progress.
- In a truly free society, those with superior abilities will naturally prosper and rise to the top of that society. This is often described as a **meritocracy**.

> **Meritocracy** A principle that suggests that although inequality is natural in a free society, in a just society those with greater abilities, drive, creativity and work ethics deserve more rewards than those who do not have those qualities.

The economy

REVISED

Typical liberal attitudes towards the economy include the following:

- Liberals see the possession of private property and the pursuit of property ownership as a natural right.
- The ideas of eighteenth-century economist Adam Smith influenced early liberals by suggesting that free markets would promote economic activity and wealth creation.
- Liberals saw economic liberty as synonymous with liberty in general. This meant that the state was rarely justified in interfering in economic activity (save for controlling natural monopolies).
- Capitalism and free trade will automatically lead to the creation of wealth, and individuals, pursuing their enlightened self-interest in a free economy, will naturally take advantage of free markets.

Exam practice answers and quick quizzes at
www.hoddereducation.co.uk/myrevisionnotesdownloads

Now test yourself

TESTED

1 Identify two liberal principles or ideas about the four key themes of study.
   (a) Human nature.
   (b) Society.
   (c) The economy.
   (d) The state.

Answers on p. 106

Differing views and tensions

Classical liberalism

REVISED

The term 'classical liberalism' refers to the kind of liberal thought that flourished in England in the first three-quarters of the nineteenth century. Its leading exponents were John Stuart Mill (1806–73 — see also p. 10) and Herbert Spencer (1820–1903). The main ideas of classical liberalism include these:

- Classical liberalism is based on **negative freedom**. This is the idea that the highest form of freedom is freedom from constraint. This implies freedom from oppressive government and laws, and freedom from external threats such as crime and exploitation.

- It is also based on the idea of the minimal state. The minimal state is one which performs only functions which can be justified in the promotion of negative liberty. In essence, such a state should confine itself to defending the nation, maintaining law and order and controlling excessive monopoly power. Nineteenth-century extreme classical liberals such as Samuel Smiles (1812–1904) and Herbert Spencer were prime examples of writers who proposed this kind of economic philosophy.

- The classical liberal idea of equal rights extended to all sections of society other than individuals whose behaviour might threaten the peace of society. Equal rights were to extend also to women and to the followers of all religions. Mary Wollstonecraft (1759–97) and Harriet Taylor (1807–58), who became Mill's wife, were prominent early liberal advocates of women's rights.

- Classical liberals supported **laissez-faire capitalism**. This is the principle that free-market capitalism is the best way of creating and spreading wealth and that the state is not justified in interfering with its free operation.

- Classical liberals, notably Smiles and Spencer, argued that, in general, people succeed or fail owing to their own efforts and that their position in society is entirely in their own hands. The state, therefore, should not attempt to intervene when individuals become dependent on welfare. This kind of anti-welfare attitude also makes for a more dynamic society, they argued.

> **Negative freedom** A conception of liberty or freedom which sees it as meaning an absence of constraint. Liberal philosopher Isaiah Berlin (1909–97) described this as 'freedom from' rather than 'freedom to'.

> **Laissez-faire capitalism** A principle mostly associated with the state's role in capitalism, which proposes that capitalism and wealth creation will be enhanced if the state does not interfere in product, financial and labour market mechanisms.

Key thinker

Mary Wollstonecraft (1759–97)

Wollstonecraft's most important publication, *A Vindication of the Rights of Woman* (1792), is still strongly linked to feminist ideology. Yet her arguments were actually rooted in liberal philosophy.

The main ideas of Mary Wollstonecraft were as follows:

- In accordance with Enlightenment belief, Wollstonecraft believed that people were rational and that human nature was naturally good, displaying sympathy and empathy for one's fellow men and women.

- She argued that women were as capable of rational thought as men.
- The free exercise of individualism (by women as well as men) was essential if society was to progress culturally and economically.
- All citizens should enjoy equality under the law and be free from discrimination.
- Specifically referring to women, she argued that they were largely to blame (alongside men) for their inferior position because they had historically accepted the superiority of men.

Key thinker

John Stuart Mill (1806–73)

Many people consider Mill to be one of the greatest philosophers England has known.

The main ideas of John Stuart Mill were as follows:

- He believed in a kind of freedom called **'negative liberty'**. This meant that each individual should be free to take whatever actions they judged fit, provided this did no harm to others. This was known as the **harm principle**.
- He distinguished between **'self-regarding'** and **'other regarding'** actions. The former should not be subject to any restriction, while the latter should be if they may cause harm to others. This led to a strong belief in tolerance of the views and actions of others.
- He believed that individual liberty was essential for the development of the individual in terms of creativity, culture and intellect.
- If individuals were able to develop their individualism, the whole of society would benefit.
- He opposed popular democracy, where the interests of the few could be crushed by the interests of the majority. As an alternative, he supported the idea of representative democracy, with, as Locke had said, limited government. For Mill, government should interfere as little as practicable in society, especially in economic activity.

Typical mistake

Liberals do not support democracy unconditionally and it is a mistake to assume they do. Liberals are suspicious of popular democracy, as expressed through referendums, on the grounds that the majority may tyrannise minorities. They also believe that representative democracy should be supported only if it represents all sections of society equally and is fully accountable to the people.

Harm principle The idea that the state is justified in interfering with individual freedom only when it is to prevent some citizens doing harm to others.

Revision activity

Revise the following principles of classical liberalism:
- the harm principle
- self-regarding actions
- negative liberty
- laissez-faire capitalism.

Exam practice answers and quick quizzes at
www.hoddereducation.co.uk/myrevisionnotesdownloads

Modern liberalism

Modern liberalism should be divided into so-called 'new liberalism', 'welfare liberalism' and 'contemporary liberalism'.

New liberalism

New liberalism included the following principles and ideas:

- Its principal advocate, T.H. Green (1836– 82), suggested that the pursuit of liberty should include not only 'negative liberty' but also what Berlin later called **positive liberty**. This was the promotion of opportunities for individuals to achieve self-realisation, the achievement of their aspirations. The state, albeit in a limited way, could foster such positive liberty.
- Individuals have a moral obligation to help each other, so positive action by the state can be justified if it is designed to help individuals achieve their goals.
- The principal way in which the state can help individuals is in providing universal education so as to create **equality of opportunity**.

> **Positive liberty** A conception of liberty or freedom which sees it in terms of the ability of the individual to achieve their aspirations and to pursue the kind of life they have freely chosen. It does not mean the absence of constraints but rather the creation of positive aids to individual freedom.
>
> **Equality of opportunity** Liberals accept that inequality is inevitable in a free society. However, they also recognise that some individuals enjoy unnatural advantages, especially related to which social class they are born into. This is seen as unjust. Liberals therefore insist on equality of opportunity, which can be achieved in two ways — education for all and the destruction of artificial privilege based on an accident of birth.

Typical mistake

When confronted with the term 'modern' or 'new' liberalism, many students believe this is limited to contemporary liberal beliefs. In fact, it refers to liberalism which emerged in the latter part of the nineteenth century in competition with classical liberalism. It therefore refers to post-classical liberalism, welfare liberalism and modern contemporary liberalism.

- New liberals also accepted that the state should provide some degree of welfare to help those with no other means of support and who were in such a position through no fault of their own.
- Followers of Green, such as L.T. Hobhouse (1864–29) and J.A. Hobson (1854–1940), went further in suggesting that equality should not just be foundational but should also extend to equality in terms of economic and social treatment.
- Hobson and Hobhouse suggested the state should play a more positive role in promoting social justice.

Table 1.1 outlines classical and new liberal principles.

Table 1.1 The transition from classical to new liberalism

Classical liberal principle	New liberal response
Negative liberty has the highest social value.	Positive liberty is as important as negative liberty.
Individuals should be free to pursue their self-interest.	Individuals have a moral obligation to care for the welfare of others.
The state should have minimal powers and functions.	In some circumstances the state should intervene to create equality of opportunity and provide welfare for those unable to care for themselves.
Free-market capitalism should be allowed to flourish and should not be regulated by the state.	Laissez-faire and free markets can lead to exploitation, deprivation and excessive inequality, so the state can be justified in intervening under some circumstances.

Welfare liberalism

Welfare liberalism added the following ideas and actions:
- The main development was the idea that it was not just government and laws that limited freedom but also adverse social and economic conditions. This idea was associated with William Beveridge, whose 1942 report led to the creation of the welfare state in Britain.
- The state was justified in providing welfare in order to alleviate the curtailment of social and economic freedom. The great evils of unemployment, low incomes, destitution in old age, chronic illness and homelessness should be reduced through welfare in order to enhance general freedom.
- The compulsory nature of the welfare state (i.e. all must contribute through taxation) could be justified on the grounds that it would enhance such freedom and would create 'social good'.
- Financing welfare from taxation would conform to social justice as contributions would be based on a person's ability to pay.

> **Exam tip**
>
> Remember that liberal ideals have flourished in several different political parties and movements in modern democracies. You should therefore include some ideas of socialism, social democracy and even conservatism when describing liberal principles and beliefs.

Contemporary liberalism

Contemporary liberalism describes what liberalism is today. It is also often described as social liberalism. It includes the following principles and ideas:
- Liberals still see freedom as the primary value.
- **Tolerance** is a key value which is associated with freedom.
- Modern social liberals subscribe to **mechanistic theory** — that social problems can be solved using rational solutions and do not require ideological transformation.
- Contemporary liberals are concerned to ensure that strong constitutional rules exist to control the power of government and to preserve citizens' rights. Where power is over-concentrated in a few hands or where government is insufficiently accountable, liberals support constitutional reform.
- The protection of human rights, both domestically and globally, is a major concern for contemporary liberals.
- The spread of education and welfare provision leads to the idea of the **enabling state**, a state that helps people ultimately to help themselves.
- Modern liberals are concerned that all sections of society should receive equal treatment by the state and by the law, and that discrimination of any kind should be outlawed and combatted by social action and cultural change. Thus, they champion the cause of women's equality and anti-discrimination with regard to ethnic minorities, the LGBTQ community, the disabled, the old, etc. Feminist Betty Friedan (1921–2006) was an early pioneer of women's equality.
- Those liberals who are seen as 'progressive' and who exist within British political parties other than the Liberal Democrats, notably the Labour, Conservative, Green and Scottish National parties, also subscribe to the social democratic ideal of social justice. Social justice encompasses equality of opportunity, a stress on state welfare and some redistribution of income from rich to poor. The concept of **distributive justice**, as developed by John Rawls (1921–2002), is supported by modern progressive liberals.

Tolerance A traditional liberal idea that society should tolerate a wide range of ideas, beliefs, religions, lifestyles and ethnicity. This is based on the principle that intolerance cannot be justified as no group or individual should feel themselves superior to others. Tolerance also promotes liberty for all. The limits to tolerance include the suppression of beliefs that may damage society and forms of action that will lead to illegality.

Mechanistic theory A philosophy that suggests that although society is extremely complex, it can be explained through rational thought and research. This also suggests that social problems can be solved through rational solutions. Though it is not a specifically liberal principle, most liberals subscribe to it.

Enabling state A state that does not necessarily provide for people directly but creates the conditions where people can help themselves. Education provision for all is a key example.

Distributive justice A theory of how to achieve social justice without it resulting in an over-powerful state and a curtailment of free-market capitalism. It recognises that the state is justified in reducing inequality as long as this does not threaten the liberty of all in society.

Exam practice answers and quick quizzes at
www.hoddereducation.co.uk/myrevisionnotesdownloads

- Progressive liberals support **multiculturalism**. This is a society where different ethnicities, religions, lifestyles and belief systems are tolerated and in which such diversity enriches society by promoting economic, social and cultural progress.
- Modern social liberals are environmentalists in that they believe that environmental damage, species depletion and exhaustion of natural resources threaten the future welfare of society.

> **Multiculturalism** Liberal multiculturalism is a belief that society is enriched by diversity, so different ethnicities, lifestyles, religions, etc. should be tolerated and celebrated.

Now test yourself

TESTED

2 Look at these prominent liberal ideas. Identify what kind of liberalism is being described. The first has been done for you.

Liberal idea	Type of liberalism
Negative liberty represents an absence of restraint and it is the highest value for liberals.	Classical liberalism
People have a moral obligation to care for the welfare of others and positive liberty is as important as negative liberty.	
Social evils and deprivation are as important curtailments of freedom as laws and over-powerful government.	
All sections of society are worthy of equal respect and should be tolerated.	
Equality of opportunity can help to ensure that all people in society achieve self-realisation.	
Constitutional reform is essential if government is to be controlled and equal rights are to be guaranteed.	

3 Explain the distinctions in views between classical and modern liberalism on these themes:
  (a) The role of the state.
  (b) Attitudes towards welfare.
  (c) Attitudes towards capitalism.

Answers on p. 106

Exam tip

Though you may not have studied multiculturalism and/or anarchism, it is worth stating in answers to questions about liberalism that both these political traditions share elements of liberalism. Multiculturalism, in particular, supports tolerance and pluralism, while anarchists stress the sovereignty of the individual, the importance of natural rights and the natural human desire for liberty.

Key thinker

John Rawls (1921–2002)

American philosopher Rawls is considered to be the most important exponent of modern liberalism in the twentieth century.

The main ideas of John Rawls were as follows:
- To the traditional liberal idea of **formal equality** Rawls added the need for equal social and political rights.
- He believed that, if asked to choose what kind of society they preferred without knowing in advance where they would stand in such a society, people would prefer a society where there is little inequality and there is equality of opportunity.

- His conception of social justice (which he called distributive justice) was that inequality in a modern capitalist-based society could be justified as long as those who do well economically do not do so at the expense of the least well off in society. In other words, we should not be allowed to prosper at the expense of others.
- He strongly supported individual liberty but insisted that freedom — formal, social and economic — should be available to all in society on an equal basis. Rawls has influenced many modern politicians on the centre-left.

Formal equality Similar to foundational equality, formal equality is a wider concept, supported by all liberals. It includes equality under the law but also the principle that every individual is entitled to equal treatment in society. It also includes the idea of equality of opportunity and the abolition of artificial social distinctions such as gender inequality and class divisions.

Typical mistake

Do not treat the socialist idea of equality as being the same as the liberal view. While socialists stress economic and social equality, liberals stress formal equality and equality of opportunity. Liberals accept that inequality, if it can be justified, is natural in a free society.

Key thinker

Betty Friedan (1921–2006)

As with all liberals, a concern for individualism lay at the heart of Friedan's philosophy.

The main ideas of Betty Friedan were as follows:
- Friedan argued strongly for individual freedom. In particular, she argued that individuals should be free to be able to achieve their potential. This kind of self-realisation was at the heart of her belief system.
- Women were the principal victims of a lack of opportunity and life choices in society. This was owing to patriarchy and dominant patriarchal attitudes.
- Friedan was adamant that if the state was based on liberal principles, it would be possible to achieve equality of opportunity for both women and men.
- She did not see the state as the principal vehicle of patriarchy, blaming dominant cultural attitudes instead.

Revision activity

Why are feminists also considered to be liberals? Consider the following feminists:
1 Mary Wollstonecraft.
2 Betty Friedan.

Exam practice answers and quick quizzes at
www.hoddereducation.co.uk/myrevisionnotesdownloads

Now test yourself

TESTED

4 Look at these prominent liberal ideas. Identify a key thinker who would have expounded such a view.

Liberal idea	Example of a key thinker
Inequality can be justified if it does not result in the worst off in society becoming even more deprived.	
The state is the result of a social contract between government and the people.	
Representative democracy is superior to popular democracy.	
All members of society should have the same opportunities, including women.	
The state is justified in creating laws only if they are designed to prevent some people doing harm to others through their actions.	
Welfare supplied by the state can be justified if it guarantees distributive justice.	

5 Explain the distinction between negative and positive liberty.

Answers on p. 106

Neo-liberalism

REVISED

Neo-liberalism is a curious variety of liberalism as, though it appears to be a modern form of classical liberalism, it is usually seen as an aspect of modern, New Right conservatism. The reason it flourishes among conservatives is that it is reactionary, proposing a return to nineteenth-century values. Its main features are these:

- It was part of the revival of New Right ideas in the late 1970s and 1980s, largely in Britain and the USA.
- Neo-liberals argue that free-market capitalism is essential for social and economic progress.
- The state should not interfere with free markets as this will inhibit economic activity and wealth creation. Thus neo-liberals support the **minimal state**.
- They oppose the 'dependency culture' whereby if welfare is too freely distributed by the state, people will become used to relying on state benefits and they will cease to be dynamic economic actors.
- Neo-liberals support free trade and globalisation.

Minimal state A concept associated with classical liberalism and modern neo-liberalism. It suggests that in a free society, the state must be strongly controlled and should have a minimal breadth of functions. If the state has too many functions it is likely to interfere with individual liberties. It is also associated with laissez-faire capitalism.

Now test yourself

TESTED

6 Briefly answer these questions about liberalism.
  (a) Why are neo-liberals described as conservatives?
  (b) Why do modern liberals support constitutional reform?
  (c) Why is Betty Friedan considered to be a liberal thinker?
  (d) How does positive liberty differ from negative liberty?
  (e) What was William Beveridge's contribution to liberalism?
  (f) Why did John Stuart Mill oppose popular democracy?

Answers on pp. 106–7

Exam tip

If you describe 'neo-liberalism' or 'libertarianism' as part of the broad liberal ideology, always state that you understand that these two doctrines are also often described as 'conservative'. Neo-liberalism and libertarianism are modern forms of classical liberalism but also branches of contemporary conservatism.

Revision activity

Briefly distinguish between these forms of liberalism:
- New liberalism.
- Welfare liberalism.
- Neo-liberalism.

Tensions within liberalism

The following are the main tensions that exist among different strands of liberal thought. In each case they are linked to one of the four key themes of human nature, society, the economy and the state.

- **Human nature.** The original liberal position is that all human beings are naturally rational and will always obey natural laws, as they see this as being in their self-interest. Modern liberals have a somewhat less optimistic view and believe that human beings have the potential to be rational and to prefer good actions over bad actions (in terms of harming others). This potential must be fostered by education and by the creation of a free, progressive society.
- **Society.** Early liberals, classical liberals and neo-liberals all lay less stress on society and more on individualism, an atomistic society and the pursuit of enlightened self-interest. Modern liberals, however, see society as more organic and believe that individuals must control their self-interest in the interests of social cohesion.
- **The economy.** Early liberals and neo-liberals favour an economy based on free market, free competition and little or no economic regulation by the state. Modern liberals, however, believe that free-market capitalism leads to too much deprivation and inequality. They therefore see state interference as justified in order to promote social welfare and to ensure social justice.
- **The state.** Since its emergence in the eighteenth century, liberalism has gradually changed its attitude to the state. Earlier liberals feared the power of the state, saw it as a threat to liberty and believed it could inhibit enterprise and reduce the dynamism of the economy. Modern liberals accepted an increasingly expanded state, notably in the fields of welfare, education and redistribution of income. This has been opposed by modern neo-liberals.

These different views are summed up in Table 1.2.

Table 1.2 A summary of how classical and modern liberals differ in their outlook on four themes

Theme	Classical liberal outlook	Modern liberal outlook
Human nature	Individuals are rational or capable of rationality and prefer to pursue their enlightened self-interest.	Individuals crave freedom but also understand that they have obligations to help others less fortunate.
Society	Society is naturally competitive and is made up of free individuals pursuing their own interest.	Society should embrace a degree of social welfare and social justice. Individualism should be tempered with social action.
The economy	The economy should be based on free markets, free trade and a lack of state intervention.	The injustices thrown up by capitalism should be reduced by the state through welfare, equality of opportunity and redistribution of income.
The state	The state should be limited and controlled by government based on representative democracy.	The power of the state and government should be controlled by strong constitutional rules and robust democracy. State intervention can be justified on the grounds of social justice, equality and social welfare.

Exam practice answers and quick quizzes at
www.hoddereducation.co.uk/myrevisionnotesdownloads

Liberalism today

If we were to summarise the main ideas of liberalism in general today, we would identify the following features:

- the defence of **liberal democracy**
- the defence of human rights
- tolerance and multiculturalism
- equal rights and the rule of law
- government limited by law and internal checks and balance
- state welfare
- social justice
- environmental concern
- mildly regulated capitalism.

> **Liberal democracy** A political system where key principles are that the rule of law applies, the government follows constitutional rules, government and elected representatives are accountable to the people, rights are safeguarded, regular free elections take place and there is a peaceful transition of power from one government to the next.

Now test yourself

7 Identify the key term associated with liberalism in each of these cases:
   (a) A kind of freedom that leads to self-realisation.
   (b) A state with very limited functions.
   (c) Free-market economics.
   (d) Giving all citizens equal life chances from birth.
   (e) All citizens enjoy equal rights and equal treatment.
   (f) An agreement between government and the governed.
   (g) A society where all people receive the rewards they deserve.
8 Explain the conflicts within liberalism between freedom and equality.

Answers on p. 107

Exam practice

You must use appropriate thinkers you have studied to support your answer and consider both sides in a balanced way.
1 To what extent do liberals disagree over the role of the state? [24]
2 To what extent do liberals support equality? [24]
3 To what extent have modern liberals abandoned the concept of negative liberty in favour of the concept of positive liberty? [24]

Answers and quick quiz 1 online

Summary

You should now have an understanding of:
- the distinction between negative and positive liberty
- liberalism's changing attitude to the state
- all aspects of the transition from classical to modern liberalism
- the relationship between liberalism and democracy, both positive and negative
- why modern liberals are heavily concerned with constitutionalism — you must be able to illustrate your answers to questions on this theme
- the contribution of at least the five key thinkers to the development of liberal thought.

2 Conservatism

The origins of conservatism

- Conservatives seek to conserve society and are distrustful of ideological thinking. Traditional conservatism emerged in part as a reaction to the rational principles of the Enlightenment.
- Therefore, conservatives have argued that pragmatism, empiricism and tradition are far superior with regard to maintaining an organic society. Humans are incapable of rationalism because they are imperfect.
- One-nation conservatives and Christian democrats both draw upon the idea of the state, led by a political elite, making small adjustments in the running of society and the economy as necessary to adapt to an ever-changing world.
- The New Right, a philosophical marriage between neo-liberalism and neo-conservativism, emerged as a force in the 1970s.
- The New Right argued that one-nation conservatives and Christian democrats had sanctioned far too many changes to the role of the state in its interactions with society and the economy, and had lost touch with true conservative values.
- Neo-liberals drew upon classical liberalism and neo-conservatives upon traditional conservatism for their respective inspirations.
- Neo-liberals are alone within conservatism in placing principle over pragmatism.

> **Typical mistake**
>
> Remember not to confuse the UK's Conservative Party with conservatism. Political parties are a mixture of different ideas, so although the Conservative Party contains lots of conservative ideas, it also espouses ideas from liberal, socialist, feminist and environmental traditions.

Core ideas of conservatism

Human nature

REVISED

Thomas Hobbes is a key figure for conservatives in understanding human nature and human imperfection. In his most famous work, *Leviathan* (1651), he argued, 'Humans are driven by a perpetual and restless desire of power.'

Noel O'Sullivan has argued that traditional conservatism is 'a philosophy of human imperfection'. Human beings are characterised as follows:
- Morally imperfect: inherently selfish creatures motivated by base desires and impulses. This concept is linked to the idea of 'original sin' from the Bible.
- Intellectually imperfect: reality is beyond their rational understanding.
- Psychologically imperfect: security driven and socially dependent, humans rely on tradition and culture for an identity and rootedness.

Neo-conservatives agree with Hobbes that human imperfection is innate and cannot be transformed. Consequently, conservatives traditionally emphasise:
- authority through strong law and order to deter criminal behaviour
- foreign policy based on national security rather than more liberal notions of cooperation.

Exam practice answers and quick quizzes at
www.hoddereducation.co.uk/myrevisionnotesdownloads

Traditional conservatives and one-nation conservative thinkers like Edmund Burke and Michael Oakeshott agree with Hobbes that humans are imperfect, but argue that society can mitigate this. However, the neo-liberal branch of the New Right has a more positive view of human nature. Neo-liberals such as Ayn Rand argue that individuals are capable of rational thought and therefore reject **human imperfection** as espoused by the other branches of conservatism.

Neo-liberals therefore see no need for an organic society with its constraints on individual freedom. Instead, they argue for:

- egotistical individualism where the rights of the individual are more important than those of the state and freedom is associated with self-interest and self-reliance
- negative freedom — individuals should be free from as many external constraints as possible. Society should be **atomistic** and not organic.

Human imperfection
The belief that humans are flawed morally, intellectually and psychologically, which limits the efficacy of the decisions they make. Therefore, doctrines or ideologies designed by humans will be inherently flawed and are not to be trusted.

Atomism Society exists as a loose collection of self-interested and self-sufficient individuals.

Key thinker

Thomas Hobbes (1588–1679)

Hobbes, one of England's most important political thinkers, took the view that human nature was driven by self-interest.

The main ideas of Thomas Hobbes were as follows:
- Humans are needy, vulnerable and easily led astray in attempts to understand the world around them. Their drives are individualistic and not communal.
- Without government and the structure of society, humans would be forced to live in a violent state of nature.
- Such a state of nature would be **'a state of war'**, a world where humans cared only about self-preservation.

- The solution to this dystopia was order and this could be achieved only by a social compact involving the individuals of society and the head of state, namely the monarch.
- This compact gave the sovereign legitimacy to pass legislation as they saw fit.
- In return for individuals ceding freedoms they would be given legal and physical protection as the rule of law would ensure order. Individuals would be bound to follow these laws.
- Society should therefore balance the need for order and the human need to live a free life. Strong authoritative government, Hobbes argued, guarantees this equilibrium.

Society

REVISED

Core ideas include the following:
- Conservatives have traditionally believed in a **hierarchical**, stable, organic society of various interlinked local communities.
- Emile Durkheim argues that individuals isolated from society suffer anomie (isolation and a sense of meaningless).
- Property rights provide stability; bequeathing and inheriting property links past, present and future.
- Conservatives argue that society cannot be contrived or created but rather emerges organically, like a living organism.
- Michael Oakeshott argues that conservatives prefer the status quo of traditions but will, as Edmund Burke argues, 'change to conserve' in order to avoid social disorder or revolution.
- **Radical** change should be avoided as it will deviate too much from tried and trusted tradition and experience. Rationalism should not be trusted.

Hierarchy Conservative belief that society is naturally organised into fixed and unequal tiers, where one's position or status is unconnected to individual ability.

Radical Any ideas that favour drastic political, economic and social change from the existing status quo.

- Traditional conservatives, one-nation conservatives, Christian democrats and New Right neo-conservatives argue that society can carefully (and not radically) change, guided by tradition, pragmatism, **empiricism**, hierarchy and Judaeo-Christian morality.
- Burke argues that society must be able to **change to conserve** itself.
- These same branches of conservatism argue that the ruling class has a paternalistic responsibility or *noblesse oblige* to society's weaker elements and to maintain equilibrium.
- Conservatives value tradition and empiricism because they assist in the maintenance of the organic society. Inherited patterns of thought and action such as social customs and religious practice inform humans past, present and future.

A different conservative view of society

Neo-liberalism, a strand of the New Right, challenges many of the traditional conservative beliefs in society:

- It believes in an atomistic society over an organic society.
- Individuals are more important than society and their freedoms are restricted by the duties and social obligations that an organic society views as essential.
- Neo-liberals are principled, preferring reason to tradition and empiricism in understanding society and making changes.

However, neo-liberal Robert Nozick concedes that humans are 'pack animals' who enjoy and need social and economic interactions.

> **Empiricism** The idea that knowledge and evidence come from real experience and not abstract theories.
>
> **Change to conserve** Society should adapt to shifting circumstances by instigating small modifications to compensate rather than rejecting change outright. These compromises will preserve the essence of society. If society does not change, it risks rebellion and/or revolution.
>
> **Noblesse oblige** The duty of the society's elite, the wealthy and privileged, to look after those less fortunate.

Key thinker

Edmund Burke (1729–97)

Edmund Burke was a key figure for conservatism as his ideas rebutted the rationalism favoured by Enlightenment thinkers.

The main ideas of Edmund Burke were as follows:

- Tradition and empiricism should be passed down through generations, as society is a partnership between **'those who are living, those who are dead and those who are to be born'**.
- However, sometimes society must change to conserve, guided by history and empiricism.
- The ruling class has a paternalistic responsibility or noblesse oblige to society's weaker elements and to maintain equilibrium.
- Burke argued that the revolution in France was a consequence of a corrupt aristocracy failing in noblesse oblige and therefore unable to change.
- The French aristocracy's devotion to Hobbesian autocracy proved disastrous. Burke argued that **'a state without the means of some change is without the means of its conservation'**.

- It is for this reason that Burke was sympathetic towards the American Revolution. He argued that the American colonists had legitimate grievances. Although America overturned British rule, it did not, unlike the French revolutionaries, abandon the values, culture, institutions and traditions of its society.
- Burke was therefore critical of the Jacobins' quest for an ideal society during the French Revolution. Instead of trusting in tradition and empiricism for guidance, they overturned the social order for Rousseau and Paine's abstract theory of the rights of humans.
- The French Revolution, based on noble abstract principles, discarded empiricism and tradition for utopian idealism, and **'philosophical abstractions'** descended disastrously into violence.
- Rather than defend the rights of humankind, it achieved the opposite because all of French society, both good and bad, was destroyed.
- As Jesse Norman has argued, what mattered to Burke was the preservation and improvement of society.

Exam practice answers and quick quizzes at
www.hoddereducation.co.uk/myrevisionnotesdownloads

Now test yourself

TESTED

1 Describe what traditional conservatives mean by an organic society.
2 Define 'pragmatism' and explain why conservatives are divided over it.
3 What do neo-liberals understand by an atomistic society?

Answers on p. 107

The state

REVISED

Thomas Hobbes believed in a social compact where individuals traded some individual freedoms for the state's protection. All branches of conservatism, apart from the neo-liberal strand of the New Right, argue the following:

- Society is not equal and has a natural hierarchy. Therefore the state, controlled by the ruling class, has a paternalistic responsibility or noblesse oblige to society's weaker elements to maintain equilibrium, like parents acting in the best interests of their children.
- Noblesse oblige adheres to Judaeo-Christian morality. It is also a pragmatic belief — if the state fails to counter societal problems, it risks the established order collapsing.
- Burke's idea of 'changing to conserve' influenced traditional conservatism and continued to develop, seeing the state intervening ever more in both society and the economy in the late nineteenth and the twentieth centuries through one-nation conservatism and Christian democrat policies.
- Traditional conservatives and neo-conservatives are organic **authoritarians** who believe in a strong state that enforces law and order, upholds traditional values and oversees a society bound by a common culture.
- One-nation conservatives and Christian democrats are organic paternalists who uphold law and order but prefer welfarism for dealing with social disorder and societal disquiet.
- Neo-conservatives, one-nation Conservatives and Christian democrats accept the need for noblesse oblige and welfare provision.
- However, neo-conservatives dislike the dependency culture that they associate with welfare and are far less generous than the other two branches of conservatism (e.g. favouring means-tested benefits, cutting disability benefits).
- Neo-conservatives' authoritarian ideas lead to them supporting hawkish interventionist foreign policy.
- One-nation conservatives' and Christian democrats' ideas lead to them supporting dovish conciliatory foreign policy.

Authoritarian The view that those in the higher positions of society are best positioned and able to make decisions on society's behalf. Their authority comes naturally from their superior position within the hierarchy and is legitimised by the obligation of those below to obey.

The neo-liberal branch of the New Right offers a different view of the state:

- Neo-liberals like Robert Nozick argue for a minimal state which maintains domestic order, enforces legal contracts and provides defence against foreign attack.
- Neo-liberals argue that the state's primary responsibility is to protect the negative freedom of the citizens.
- They maintain that the state should not infringe personal liberty, and believe in negative freedom on issues such as sexuality, abortion and recreational drug taking.
- Neo-liberals argue that economic, moral and welfare issues are the concerns of the individual and not the state. This will increase individual freedom and personal responsibility, as Ayn Rand strongly advocates.
- They argue that the taxation needed to fund the state's spending infringes individual liberty and creates a dependency culture.
- Neo-liberals fear the larger active state favoured by other branches of conservatism: Friedrich von Hayek, Robert Nozick and Ayn Rand believe that the growth of the state is the gravest contemporary threat to individual freedom.

Key thinker

Ayn Rand (1905–82)

Ayn Rand is an unusual political thinker as many of her philosophical ideas are found in works of fiction, in particular *Atlas Shrugged* (1957).

The main ideas of Ayn Rand were as follows:
- She believed in **'objectivism'**, whose core beliefs are:
  - ○ an atomistic society where individuals enjoy negative freedom
  - ○ only when individuals comprehend the true nature of reality can they independently achieve self-realisation and self-fulfilment
  - ○ individuals are rational and their highest moral purpose is the achievement of personal happiness.
- Rand rejected human imperfection as espoused by most branches of conservatism: **'man must be the beneficiary of his own moral actions'**.

- She loathed organic society because the obligations demanded from individuals eroded their freedoms.
- The only moral purpose of society is to protect individual rights.
- Individuals must maintain their lives through their own efforts. Rand opposed welfare provision.
- Individuals have the right to maintain property and income without being taxed for welfare spending.
- Rand feared the state interfering in individuals' lives. State interference was the product of a flawed understanding of altruism.
- Her belief in negative liberty provides the philosophical justification for **'rolling back the state'**, not just economically but in social matters such as homosexuality and abortion.
- Rand was not an anarchist as she required a small state to maintain free markets and social laissez-faire and to defend borders.

Typical mistake

Ayn Rand was only against state welfare provision if it was state sponsored. If individuals *chose* to donate money to charities providing social welfare (known as 'voluntarism'), that was fine with Rand as it was an individual's choice and not a state obligation that was limiting their freedom.

Exam practice answers and quick quizzes at
www.hoddereducation.co.uk/myrevisionnotesdownloads

Key thinker

Robert Nozick (1938–2002)

Nozick's most famous work, *Anarchy, State and Utopia* (1974), was a rebuttal to liberal philosopher John Rawls' attempts to reconcile liberal individualism (which Nozick approved of) with principles of redistribution and social justice (which Nozick disagreed with) in *A Theory of Justice* (Rawls, 1970).

The main ideas of Robert Nozick were as follows:

- He was initially influenced by John Locke's rationalism, which focused on the individual rights of men, and Kant's idea that individuals in society cannot be treated as a thing or used as a resource.
- Nozick therefore argued for self-ownership, meaning that individuals own their bodies, talents, abilities and labour. This led him to two broad conclusions:
  - Miniaturist government with minimal interference in the lives of individuals makes for the best society.
  - The state's primary function is to protect individual human rights, with its involvement 'limited to the narrow functions of force, theft, enforcement of contracts and so on'.
- Nozick disagreed with Hobbes', Burke's and Oakeshott's belief that the state had legitimacy to interfere in society based on a hierarchical social contract. Rather than reinforcing individual freedoms, such state interference did the opposite.
- The state has too much power over personal freedom: **'The state's claim to legitimacy induces its citizens to believe they have some duty to obey its edict, pay its taxes, fight its battles, and so on'.**
- Nozick was critical of taxation: **'Taxation of earnings from labour is on a par with forced labour'.**
- Nozick was critical of the state determining welfare: **'The illegitimate use of a state by economic interests for their own end is based upon a pre-existing illegitimate power of the state to enrich some persons at the expense of others'.**

The economy

REVISED

Capitalism is a system that leads to economic inequality, in keeping with traditional conservative ideas of the hierarchical nature of society and state. Traditional conservative thinkers like Burke supported free-market economists like Adam Smith.

- All conservatives regard private property as a vital component of the economy as it provides psychological security for individuals within society, especially during economic recessions and depression.
- Private property provides moral wellbeing that is appreciated by all branches of conservatism, aiding self-actualisation — individuals can see themselves in their property.
- Private property gives individuals a stake in society, be it an atomistic society, as favoured by neo-liberalism, or an organic society, as favoured by the rest of conservatism.
- Economically, private property reduces individuals' dependency upon the state.
- Most conservatives argue that private property strengthens social cohesion.

However, traditional and one-nation conservatives have an ambivalent attitude towards the economy and have sometimes been dubbed 'reluctant supporters' of capitalism. They are sceptical about the doctrinal elements of **laissez-faire** classical/neo-liberal theory.

- Traditional conservatives' scepticism over laissez-faire economics in the early nineteenth century saw them introduce protectionist tariffs to shelter society and the economy from the vagaries of the market.

> **Laissez-faire** A belief in the free-market capitalist economy and minimal state intervention in economic, social and political spheres.

- Likewise, one-nation conservatives and Christian democrats of the twentieth century were enticed by Keynesian economics, whereby the state would manage the market on paternalistic terms with the goal of full employment.

Inevitably, neo-liberals disagree with such deviations from classical liberalism, rejecting paternalism and being wholly committed to:
- laissez-faire market economics and negative economic freedom
- 'a rolling back' of the state's involvement in society
- abolishing expensive welfare states and the dependency culture they create
- deregulation and privatisation of all services
- obstructive bodies to the free market, like trade unions, having their powers curtailed.

Neo-liberals are radical — they favour drastic political, economic and social change to the organisation of state and society based upon ideological doctrines.

Differing views and tensions

Traditional conservatism

REVISED

Traditional conservatism has its origins in the late eighteenth century as a reaction to both the Enlightenment and the consequences of the French Revolution. The key text is Edmund Burke's *Reflections on the Revolution in France* (1790). Burke sets out a template for traditional conservatism that defends the established order and how change will sometimes be necessary to maintain the status quo. For this reason, Burke is a key thinker for both traditional and one-nation conservatism.

The main ideas of traditional conservatism include the following:
- For imperfect humans, the state, as Thomas Hobbes argued, provides the authority necessary to act as a break on individuals' worst instincts.
- Society is hierarchical and unequal. Burke argues that the state's elite has a paternal responsibility, or a noblesse oblige, to maintain society and govern in the interests of the people.
- Society is organised this way because humans do not have the same abilities, talents or energy; occupations are differentiated by skill and ability, and financial rewards (wages) are decided by the supply and demand of the market.
- Traditional conservatives view society's elite as being the natural leaders and believe that other social groups should accept their ability to lead in the best interests of society as a whole.
- Therefore the state, led by the elite, has a natural authority with a disciplinary function to provide order, security and stability to society.
- When necessary, society can carefully (and not radically) change, guided by tradition, pragmatism, empiricism, hierarchy and Judaeo-Christian morality.
- Traditional conservatives view humans as intellectually imperfect and incapable of the infallible rational thought promised by political ideas such as those of liberals.
- Society is not contrived or created but rather emerges organically, like a living organism. Society's development cannot be predicted, only responded to.

Burke believed revolutionary France was a contrived society based on rational liberal ideas rather than traditions. Its failure was a consequence of human imperfection and intellectual fallibility. He viewed human imperfection as a reason why change should not be entered into lightly: **'What has stood the test of time is good and must not be lightly cast aside.'**

Writing in the twentieth century, Michael Oakeshott illustrates the traditional conservative position with this quote: **'To be conservative, then, is to prefer the familiar to the unknown, to prefer the tried to the untried, fact to mystery, the actual to the possible, the limited to the unbound…present laughter to utopian bliss.'**

> **Typical mistake**
>
> Do not confuse Oakeshott's 'politics of faith' with religious faith. Rather, Oakeshott is criticising what he perceives as a misguided faith in rationalism and ideology.

Key thinker

Michael Oakeshott (1901–90)

Michael Oakeshott's key text is *On Being Conservative* (1962).

The main ideas of Michael Oakeshott were as follows:
- The politics of faith: because of human imperfection it is beyond the ability of human beings to understand reality.
- Modern society is unpredictable and multi-faceted. Faith in rationalism is therefore misplaced as theories often oversimplify complex situations.
- Therefore Oakeshott was critical of a leader acting on the **'authority of his own reason'** rather than experience.
- The politics of scepticism: rationalism and its doctrines are therefore worthless and humans should put their faith in trusted traditions and empiricism.

- Like Burke, Oakeshott believed that change should be informed carefully and guided by pragmatism and empiricism so that **'the cure is not worse than the disease'** and will maintain social stability.
- The security of longstanding customs and traditions is at the core of his conservative ideas and he held deep distrust for unproven promises of abstract theories.
- Pragmatism is flexible and can acknowledge complex and altering realities in a way that rigid rationalist ideologies cannot. Likewise, it can deliver what is in the best interests of the people.
- Whereas Burke used the French Revolution as an example of the disastrous consequences of following rationalism, Oakeshott argued that violent fascist and communist regimes were the twentieth century's examples of flawed rationalism.

One-nation conservatism

REVISED

One-nation conservatism emerged in the late nineteenth century, updating Burke's idea that society needed to change to conserve. British prime minister Benjamin Disraeli felt that society was threatened by the social and economic consequences of the industrial revolution: increasing class inequality and a declining sense of community. Disraeli embraced paternalism and social reform acting in the interests of everyone and preserving one nation. One-nation conservatism developed in the twentieth century under Harold Macmillan and its ideas are still present within the conservatism of recent prime ministers David Cameron and Theresa May.

The main ideas of one-nation conservatism include the following:
- Disraeli introduced social reforms to counter the negative effects of capitalism and laissez-faire government. By using pragmatism to address social problems, he reduced the possibility of social unrest.
- Examples of the first one-nation conservative social reforms were:
  ○ the Second Reform Act, which gave working men the vote (1867)
  ○ the Artisans Dwellings Act (1875)

○ the Sale of Food and Drugs Act (1875)
○ the Conspiracy and Protection of Property Act (1875).

- German chancellor Otto von Bismarck adopted similar policies in 1889 when his government introduced the first old-age pension and the concept of mass retirement.
- In the twentieth century, one-nation conservatism continued to respond to emerging social problems.
- Post-war housing in the UK was a huge issue and Harold Macmillan succeeded in building 300,000 houses a year as Winston Churchill's housing minister.
- As prime minister between 1957 and 1963, Macmillan put into practice combined state ownership and private enterprise, which he wrote about in *The Middle Way* (1938).
- Macmillan's adoption of a mixed economy reframed Disraeli's one-nation conservatism for the twentieth century.
- Therefore, one-nation conservatives are organic paternalists who seek to solve social instability and disorder with benevolent welfarism.
- In the twenty-first century, David Cameron championed communal responsibilities, attempting to rebrand one-nation conservatism as 'compassionate conservatism' with his Big Society initiatives.
- Both Cameron and Theresa May maintained one-nation conservative values by 'changing to conserve' the UK in accepting devolution but opposing Scottish and Welsh independence.
- Theresa May demonstrates one-nation conservative values by arguing for a society that respects the 'bonds of family, community and citizenship'.

The European version of one-nation conservatism is called Christian democracy. The two strands of conservatism are very similar.

- Christian democrats are influenced by the paternalistic ideas of Friedrich List.
- Like one-nation conservatism it stresses the importance of noblesse oblige and communal duty, emphasising the importance of a 'social market' of capitalism.
- Unlike one-nation conservatives or other branches of conservatism, Christian democrats favour **supranationalism** — exemplified in the EU — where sovereignty is pooled with other nation states.

> **Revision activity**
>
> How do one-nation conservatives agree with and differ from social democrats and Third Way socialists? Consider the following socialists:
> 1 Anthony Crosland.
> 2 Anthony Giddens.

> **Supranationalism**
> Sovereignty transcending national boundaries. Within the EU, nations will often pool their sovereignty and make decisions at the European level as well as at the traditional national level. This system resembles federalism.

The New Right

REVISED

The New Right emerged in the UK and the USA in the 1970s and was a reaction against the ideas of one-nation conservatism, modern liberalism and social democracy. The New Right is formed of two strands: neo-liberalism and neo-conservatism.

- Neo-liberalism is a modernised version of classical liberalism, focused on a minimal state, an atomistic society, a free-market economy and individual freedom. Neo-liberalism's critique of government intervention gained traction in the 1970s when western governments adopting Keynesian economics struggled to cope with stagflation.
- Neo-conservatism is a modernised version of traditional conservatism, focused on morality, social order and a hawkish foreign policy. Neo-conservatives were critical of the permissive social attitudes that had become mainstream after the social revolution of the 1960s and sought a more authoritarian foreign policy, especially against communist states like the USSR.

Exam practice answers and quick quizzes at
www.hoddereducation.co.uk/myrevisionnotesdownloads

Neo-liberalism

Neo-liberalism is heavily influenced by nineteenth-century classical liberalism. Neo-liberalism ideas involve principled and doctrinaire thinking, including the following:

- Human nature is rational and self-seeking. Ayn Rand rejects the idea of human imperfection.
- Society is atomistic. Individual rights and freedom are more important than societal obligations and duties, as Robert Nozick and Ayn Rand both argue.
- Neo-liberals fear the duties and obligations present in the organic state, perceiving them as a threat to freedom. Robert Nozick and Ayn Rand both argue that individuals' obligations should be to themselves rather than to state or society.
- To preserve individual freedom, government should 'roll back the state'.
- Nozick and Rand advocate this idea, arguing that high taxation infringes individual rights and that a welfare state creates a dependency culture.
- The economy should be a free market, embracing negative freedom.
- Therefore neo-liberals do not believe in government intervention. Individuals should rise and fall based on their abilities, with no help or assistance from the state.
- Neo-liberals believe that state planning and nationalised companies worsen economic performance as they distort the free market.
- Nationalised industries are inefficient, lacking free-market dynamism and innovation, and are artificially protected from free-market competition, which distorts the overall market.
- The exception to the rule for neo-liberal intervention in the economy is regarding inflation.
- Milton Friedman argued that Keynesian policies were inflationary, which reduced economic activity. He advocated a policy called 'monetarism' to control the money supply via cuts in public spending.
- Government's primary role within the economy is to control inflation. Monetarist policies were pursued by Margaret Thatcher in the UK and Ronald Reagan in the USA during the 1980s.

Neo-conservatism

Neo-conservatism is heavily influenced by nineteenth-century traditional conservatism. Neo-conservatives (informed by Judeo-Christian values) were horrified by the social and sexual revolution of the 1960s that saw the erosion of traditional values within the organic society. Examples of neo-conservative ideas include:

- favouring pragmatism over principle
- an organic society based on Christian values and traditional marriage, arguing for **anti-permissiveness** within society
- abolition of abortion laws (particularly in the USA)
- antipathy to homosexuality and, more recently, LGBTQ rights
- recognising the need for noblesse oblige but arguing that the welfare state has grown too generous, creating a dependency culture.

New Right conservatives are organic authoritarians, preferring strict law and order to solve social instability and social disorder.

> **Anti-permissiveness**
> A rejection, informed by Judeo-Christian morality, of the relativist idea that there is no right and wrong, which neo-conservatism dubbed 'permissiveness'. Neo-conservatives argue that sex before marriage, homosexuality, abortion and recreational drug taking are wrong.

- Thatcher and Reagan both had a 'war' on recreational drug use and advocated strict prison sentences as both a moral punishment and an authoritarian deterrent.
- Neo-conservatism advocates hawkish foreign policy and military intervention to protect the security of the state:
  - in US politics with aggressive anti-Soviet (and therefore anti-communist) foreign policy
  - in UK politics with Mrs Thatcher in the Falklands War and the first Gulf War.
- More recently, President George W. Bush and Prime Minister Tony Blair's neo-conservative-inspired foreign policy saw the USA and the UK invade Afghanistan and Iraq.

Now test yourself

TESTED

4 Look at the following conservative ideas. Identify a key thinker who would have expounded such a view.
  (a) Individuals are rational and their highest moral purpose is the achievement of their personal happiness.
  (b) The state should not put its faith in scepticism rather than rationalism.
  (c) Without society, humans would live in a violent state of nature.
  (d) Individuals in society cannot be treated as a thing or used as a resource.
  (e) What has stood the test of time is good and must not be lightly cast aside.

Answers on p. 107

Exam tip

There are more than five conservative thinkers, as you have probably learned, but be selective about discussing others in your answers. The exam specification is primarily interested in the ideas of the five key thinkers and you should try to include them in your answers before you include other political thinkers.

Typical mistake

Remember to focus on the main ideas of each key thinker — biographical information might be interesting but it is not relevant to the exam question.

Now test yourself

TESTED

5 Briefly answer these questions about conservatism.
  (a) How do the organic and the atomistic society differ?
  (b) Why is Ayn Rand considered a member of the New Right and not an anarchist?
  (c) Why do conservatives disagree so strongly about rationalism?
  (d) What was Robert Nozick's contribution to conservatism?
  (e) Why do one-nation conservatives and Christian democrats support changing society?

Answers on p. 107

Revision activity

Briefly distinguish between these forms of conservatism:
1 One-nation conservatism and neo-liberalism.
2 Neo-liberalism and neo-conservatism.
3 Traditional conservatism and Christian democracy.

Exam practice answers and quick quizzes at
www.hoddereducation.co.uk/myrevisionnotesdownloads

Differing views and tensions

The following are the main tensions that exist among different strands of conservative thought.

Human nature

REVISED

- The original position of conservatism is that human beings are unequal and are morally, intellectually and psychologically imperfect, as first argued by Thomas Hobbes.
- Conservatives believe in a hierarchical, organic society where individuals are protected from their inherent selfishness by the state. They are distrustful of rationalism.
- This view is shared by traditional conservatives, one-nation conservatives, Christian democrats and New Right neo-conservatives.
- However, New Right neo-liberals have a more positive view of human nature, believing humans capable of being rational and that individualism therefore supersedes the state and society.

Typical mistake

Although neo-liberals have a positive view of human nature, do not forget that they acknowledge, as a concession to human imperfection, that there is a need for the state to enforce laws. Robert Nozick argues that the preservation of liberty *'could not be taken for granted'*.

Society

REVISED

- For imperfect humans, an organic society provides stability, security and a brake on our worst instincts. Burke and Oakeshott agree with Hobbes that humans are imperfect but that society can mitigate this.
- This view is shared by those traditional conservatives, one-nation conservatives, Christian democrats and neo-conservatives.
- Neo-liberals are at odds with the rest of conservatism because they view society as atomistic, arguing that negative freedom and individualism are more important than any obligations to society.

The state

REVISED

- Traditional conservatives' and one-nation conservatives' view of the state is that the ruling class paternally governs for the benefit of all.
- The post-war period saw the state taking an increasing role in the economy, the emergence of the welfare state and acceptance of liberal changes in society.
- Both traditional and one-nation conservatives are organic paternalists who seek to solve social instability and disorder with benevolent welfarism. One-nation conservatives continued to increase the levels of welfare provision while in government.
- The New Right opposed these changes:
  - ○ Atomistic neo-liberals objected to state intervention, which they perceived as undermining individual freedoms and creating a dependency culture.
  - ○ Neo-conservatives opposed the social and sexual revolution, which they believed eroded traditional values. Instead they championed what they called anti-permissiveness. Neo-conservatives agreed with the noblesse oblige of welfare provision but thought one-nation conservatives had been too generous and created a dependency culture.
- However, the New Right is ambivalent on social issues.
- Neo-liberals argue that the state should not infringe personal liberty and believe in negative freedom on issues such as sexuality, abortion and recreational drug taking.

- Neo-conservatives oppose all of the above because they view them as immoral.
- One-nation conservatives are paternalistic, preferring a more conciliatory foreign policy to defend nationalistic values.
- Traditional conservatives and neo-conservatives are organic authoritarians, therefore preferring a more hawkish foreign policy.
- Neo-liberals argue that the state's job is to protects its borders.
- European Christian democrats favour supranationalism — exemplified in the EU — rather than the traditional nation-state as a solution to Europe's ultra-nationalistic and war-ridden past.
- Neo-liberals prefer an atomistic society and a minimal state, and distrust federal institutions like the EU as they threaten individual freedom and autonomy.
- Traditional conservatives, one-nation conservatives and neo-conservatives are all against supranationality as it threatens national sovereignty.

Exam tip

It is easy to mix up one-nation conservatism and Christian democracy. Be clear why Christian democrats are more comfortable with supranationalism than one-nation conservatives, who prefer nationalism.

The economy

REVISED

- Traditional conservatives followed the classical liberal ideas of Adam Smith, who suggested that free markets would promote economic activity and wealth creation.
- After the Second World War both one-nation conservatives and Christian democrats subscribed to Keynesian economics, whereby the state intervened in the economy to maintain full employment and to regulate economic cycles.
- The New Right is ambivalent on the issue of the economy.
- Neo-liberals strongly disapprove of such 'big state' politics and Keynesian economics as they contradict their view of an atomistic society and laissez-faire economy while also restricting individual freedom.
- Neo-conservatives are sympathetic to the classical liberalism espoused by neo-liberals as this is what traditional conservativism believed.
- However, neo-conservatives still prefer pragmatism to principle. This was demonstrated by their support for government intervention (something neo-liberals opposed) during the economic crisis of 2008 onwards.

Typical mistake

Neo-liberals are not totally against government intervention as they believe that the state can practise monetarism (controlling the total amount of money in circulation) to prevent inflation.

Exam tip

You must understand the distinctions within the New Right between neo-conservatives and neo-liberals. You must show that you can tell the difference between these two forms of New Right conservatism.

Exam practice answers and quick quizzes at
www.hoddereducation.co.uk/myrevisionnotesdownloads

Now test yourself

6 Identify two conservative ideas about the four key themes of study.
 (a) Human nature.
 (b) Society.
 (c) The state.
 (d) The economy.
7 How and why do conservatives disagree with each other about the role of the state?
8 What is supranationalism and what are conservative attitudes towards it?
9 Why did Thomas Hobbes argue that there needed to be a social compact between the individual and the state?
10 Why was Edmund Burke sympathetic to the American War of Independence but not to the French Revolution?
11 Why was Michael Oakeshott critical of the 'politics of faith' but supportive of the 'politics of scepticism'?
12 What did Ayn Rand mean by the term 'objectivism'?
13 Identify the key terms associated with conservatism which are identified in each of these cases:
 (a) Morality and right and wrong exist and society must uphold these values.
 (b) Individuals are morally, intellectually and psychologically flawed.
 (c) There should be minimal state intervention in the running of the economy and society.
 (d) It is the duty of the ruling elite to look after those less fortunate.
 (e) Society is essentially a loose collection of self-interested and self-sufficient individuals.
 (f) There should be a drastic change from the status quo.
 (g) Those in the higher echelons of society are best positioned and able to make decisions on society's behalf.
 (h) There should be a society formed in fixed tiers.
 (i) The state must make occasional small modifications to society if it is to retain its essence.
 (j) Knowledge and understanding are gained via experience and tradition.

Answers on pp. 107–08

Exam practice

You must use appropriate thinkers you have studied to support your answer and consider both sides in a balanced way.
1 To what extent do conservatives agree about human nature? [24]
2 To what extent do conservatives disagree about the state's role in the economy? [24]
3 To what extent do conservatives agree on pragmatism? [24]

Answers and quick quiz 2 online

Summary

You should now have an understanding of:
- how conservatives' different understanding of human nature informs their attitude towards society, the state and the economy
- why traditional conservatism develops into one-nation conservatism and Christian democracy
- why in turn the New Right reacts against one-nation conservative and Christian democratic ideas
- the contribution of the five key thinkers to the development of conservative thought
- how the five key thinkers agree and disagree about human nature, the state, society and the economy.

3 Socialism

The origins of socialism

- Socialism is traditionally defined as being opposed to **capitalism** and the term was first used by utopian socialists Charles Fourier and Robert Owen in the early nineteenth century.
- Socialists disagree on their aims and their methods for effecting change:
  - Revolutionary socialism, originally derived from Marx and Engels, is also known as Marxism. It argues that socialist values cannot co-exist with capitalism and therefore a revolution is inevitable.
  - Marxism was adapted by the likes of Lenin, Stalin, Mao and Castro in a series of revolutions that saw capitalist societies replaced by societies dubbed 'communist', although none remotely resembled the communism described by Marx and Engels.
  - Social democracy emerged after the Second World War and rejected revolutionary politics, preferring **evolutionary socialism**, which sought to achieve its objectives via existing democratic constitutional means.
  - In the 1980s and 1990s the Third Way emerged as a synthesis of neo-liberal and social democratic ideas and was championed by New Labour prime ministers Tony Blair and Gordon Brown in the UK, Chancellor Gerhard Schroeder of Germany's Social Democratic Party and Bill Clinton's Democrat Party.
- Socialists value equality. Revolutionary socialists favour equality of outcome and absolute equality, while social democrats and the Third Way broadly favour equality of opportunity and equality of welfare.

> **Capitalism** An economic system, organised by the market, based on private property, free enterprise and competition between individuals and companies. Socialists are concerned that this system produces unfair and unequal economic and social consequences for individuals.
>
> **Evolutionary socialism** Rather than a radical change, via a revolution, socialism is achieved gradually within the pre-existing parliamentary structure. Socialism will therefore emerge in a gradual, piecemeal fashion via the state.

Core ideas of socialism

Human nature

REVISED

Socialists' view of human nature includes the following:
- They have an optimistic view of human nature that believes individuals possess a common humanity and are essentially rational, social creatures who naturally gravitate towards **cooperation** and sociability.
- However, human nature is not fixed but is easily shaped by an individual's environment, so human nature and human behaviour are determined by society.
- Society is capable of remodelling human nature in both positive and negative ways. Most socialists argue that capitalism has had a negative effect upon human nature as it indoctrinates selfish, individualistic and greedy behaviour.
- Marx and Engels argue that individuals are 'deformed' by capitalism because they cannot reach their true human potential.
- Beatrice Webb is the one socialist thinker with a negative view of human nature, as she regarded the average voter as selfish. This

> **Cooperation** Individuals working collectively to achieve mutual benefit in the fraternal belief that humans work best when working together for a collective goal where they can share the benefits.

explains why she was against worker control. Favouring paternalism, she preferred a representative democracy with an enlightened socialist governing class.

- Socialists do not believe that all individuals have identical abilities or needs.

Key thinkers

Karl Marx (1818–83) and Friedrich Engels (1820–95)

Marx and his collaborator, Engels, are pivotal figures within socialism. Key works like *The Communist Manifesto* (1848) and *Das Kapital* (1867) provided a radical reinterpretation of history and a revolutionary model for a utopian society.

The main ideas of Karl Marx and Friedrich Engels were as follows:

- They believed their theories were empirical and scientifically determined, so as well as explaining historical change, they believed their theories to be inevitable, i.e. they were going to happen.
- Class struggle, arising from property ownership, had existed through history and

Marx and Engels believed that history was therefore teleological, with a final destination: communism.

- Capitalism with its crises and recessions will eventually benefit only a tiny minority of the ruling class. The vast majority of individuals will form the proletariat, who will wake up to their exploitation and achieve class consciousness.
- The proletariat will overthrow capitalism and a transitional phase, the dictatorship of the proletariat, will occur.
- After a period of transition the state will wither away and a stateless communist society will emerge based on common ownership. This will be the peak of human achievement and the end of history.

Exam tip

Remember that Marx and Engels are responsible for several 'firsts' within socialist thinking: first to argue that positive human nature had been distorted by capitalism; first to critique capitalist economics; first to place social class at the heart of socialist ideas; first to argue that the state was not neutral but a puppet of the ruling class; first to articulate both the need for and the inevitability of revolution.

Typical mistake

Marx and Engels have far more to say on the nature, flaws and inevitable failure of capitalism than they do on an actual communist society. Students often forget that Marx and Engels never explained in any detail how nationalisation, production, labour or economic planning would actually work in practice.

Typical mistake

Students often think that because liberalism and socialism broadly have a positive view of human nature, they are essentially the same. This is inaccurate as liberals view human nature as rational but self-interested, while socialists view human nature as rational but altruistic.

Society

REVISED

Socialists' view of society includes the following:

- Human nature and society are closely interlinked, as individuals are products of their society. Consequently, if society is to be improved there will have to be a corresponding improvement in the behaviour of individuals.
- Social class divides society and socialists therefore believe in **social justice**. For this to be achieved there must be equality of outcome and a narrowing/eliminating of the gap between social classes.

Social justice A moral justification to redistribute wealth so as to limit inequality and provide equality of opportunity for everyone in society.

- Socialists believe in the positive capabilities of human nature and **fraternity**, which leads them to believe that humans can be stimulated by common humanity and their contributions are motivated by the improvement of society and taking responsibility for the less fortunate, as opposed to individual materialistic gratification.
- Society should be based on equality as it ensures economic fairness, reinforces collectivism and satisfies everyone's basic human needs.
- Revolutionary socialism believes society must undergo revolution to achieve the perfect society.
- Revolutionary socialists, such as Marx and Engels and Rosa Luxemburg, argue for equality of outcome where rewards are based on an individual's contribution and absolute equality where everyone who contributes to society receives the same reward.
- Revolutionary socialists argue that equality can be achieved only with the abolition of private property and the common ownership of the means of production with workers' control.
- Revolutionary socialists and democratic socialists such as Beatrice Webb argue that society should be run on collectivist lines, as morally the group should take precedence over individual self-interest.
- Social democrats are focused less on collectivism and more on reforming capitalism so that society can share the benefits of economic growth.
- Social democrats argue that, for society as a whole to benefit, there must be a mixed economy utilising **Keynesian economics** that will maintain full employment and economic growth.
- They argue that society will benefit through equality of welfare to tackle poverty.
- Likewise, social democracy thinker Anthony Crosland argued for equality of opportunity in society, with no class barriers or privileges, thus socially reforming and restructuring society.
- Third Way thinker Anthony Giddens argued for a narrower focus of equality of opportunity than social democracy, focusing on social investment within infrastructure and education.
- He argued that societal community is 'fundamental' to offset the negative effects of free-market globalisation. Community brings social cohesion, social values and social responsibility. Citizens are stakeholders within society.

> **Fraternity** The belief that humans should regard each other as siblings rather than rivals and, therefore, relationships should be based not on competition or enmity but on generosity and solidarity.
>
> **Keynesian economics** Economist John Maynard Keynes argued that governments should stimulate economic demand in times of recession via state spending. Governments should also manage the economy by using tax and interest rates to influence demand and prevent recessions.

> **Typical mistake**
>
> Students often think of collectivism as a purely socialist concept, which is a mistake. Conservatism, liberalism, nationalism and feminism all have collective aspects within their ideas.

The state

REVISED

- Revolutionary socialists see the state as a tool of the bourgeoisie, which reinforces the inequality and selfishness of capitalism. Most revolutionary socialists follow the lead of Marx and Engels, who believe that the state will no longer be needed once the communist revolution is complete.
- Conversely, democratic socialists like Beatrice Webb argue that an expansion of the state is needed to plan and enforce reforms such as equality of opportunity, equality of outcome and redistributive economic policy. Capitalism would gradually be replaced by socialism.
- Social democrats argue that the role of the state is to reform capitalism.
- Social democrats like Anthony Crosland argued that it is the state's job to deliver social equality and social justice.
- Social democrats argue that the state, utilising Keynesian economics, will manage the economy to ensure continual high employment, low inflation and growth.

> **Typical mistake**
>
> Do not assume that societies that have undergone Marxist-inspired revolutions functioned without a state. In reality, such countries, like the USSR, always maintained a powerful state to enforce their authority. This has involved sanctioned state violence and oppression, which counter the core value of socialist fraternity.

Exam practice answers and quick quizzes at
www.hoddereducation.co.uk/myrevisionnotesdownloads

- They argue that the state will use the proceeds of its wise economic management to counter capitalism's inequality via a redistribution of wealth through equality of welfare.
- Third Way socialists like Anthony Giddens argue that citizens should be stakeholders within society and that the state should undertake **'social investment'**, investing in social infrastructure such as education and training.
- The Third Way argues that the state should not do too much as it will create a dependency culture. Therefore citizens have a responsibility to take advantage of what the state is offering.
- The Third Way argues against 'top-down' state intervention, preferring free-market participation in the delivery of public services.

The economy

REVISED

Socialists' view of the economy includes the following:
- Socialists differ in their attitude to capitalism.
- Revolutionary socialists like Marx and Engels argue that capitalism distorts human consciousness and leaves the worker 'deformed', with the proletariat exploited by the bourgeoisie.
- Revolutionary and democratic socialists want capitalism abolished and replaced with an economy based on collective ownership of property and the workers controlling the means of production.
- Revolutionary socialists argue that equality can be achieved only with the abolition of private property and the common ownership of the means of production with workers' control.
- Revolutionary socialists argue that any attempts to reform capitalism will completely undermine the core objectives of socialism. Luxemburg maintains that the exploitative elements within capitalism are too strong.
- Marx and Engels argued that capitalism's innate contradictions and crises mean that its collapse is inevitable. This is a predominant theme within revolutionary socialism.
- Democratic socialist Beatrice Webb argued that equality of ownership would equate to extensive state nationalisation and not the workers taking direct control. She preferred a paternal socialist governing class.
- Social democrats disagree with revolutionary socialists and democratic socialists and argue that capitalism should not be abolished but reformed.
- Social democrats argue for a mixed economy of state and privately run industries. The state would regulate the economy using Keynesian economics to maintain growth and full employment.
- Social democrats wish to reform the inequalities of capitalism via the welfare state, which would redistribute wealth.
- Social democrats like Anthony Crosland focus on social justice rather than common ownership and emphasise that the state must manage the economy wisely so that its benefits can be shared on an egalitarian basis.
- Social democrats wish to redistribute wealth, resources and opportunities via public ownership and extensive public services that would be financed by progressive taxation.
- The Third Way embraces aspects of the free market and abandons top-down state intervention. It envisages private enterprise being involved in the delivery of public services, as in the private finance initiatives instigated by New Labour.

- The Third Way rejects the non-means-tested redistribution of wealth advocated by social democracy as Giddens argues that it leads to a dependency culture.
- The Third Way advocates what Giddens describes as a **'social investment state'** where the proceeds of economic growth are invested in the infrastructure of society (such as education and training). This would vastly improve equality of opportunity.
- The Third Way advocates equality of welfare but to a lesser extent than social democracy (it expects students to contribute to the cost of university education, for example). It argues for a regulated economy to reinforce workers' rights: minimum wage, abolition of zero-hour contracts, equal pay, maternity leave, etc.

Now test yourself

TESTED

1 Identify two socialist ideas about the four key themes of study.
  (a) Human nature.
  (b) Society.
  (c) The state.
  (d) The economy.

Answers on p. 108

Differing views and tensions

Revolutionary socialism

REVISED

The earliest form of socialism was revolutionary socialism, which sought to abolish the capitalist economy, state and society, and replace it with communism, a system based on collectivism where humans work together for the common good and society is based on **common ownership**.

The two main schools of revolutionary socialism were:
- utopian socialism
- Marxism.

Utopian socialism is by far the weaker of the two traditions, while Marxism has had by far the greatest influence on socialist thought.

Utopian socialism

- Utopian socialists were a collection of thinkers who despised the exploitation, greed and selfish individualism of capitalism. Robert Owen, Charles Fourier and Étienne Cabet all proposed different versions of a utopian society in the nineteenth century.
- Owen argued that free-market capitalism should be replaced by small-scale cooperative communities that would be communally owned.
- Fourier argued for the creation of similar communities and was also one of the first feminists arguing for an extension of rights to women.
- Marx described this form of socialism as utopian, criticising it as an idealistic and simplistic fantasy with no depth of thought as to how such a society would be created or maintained.

Common ownership
The opposite of private ownership, which exists in the free-market capitalist economy. It is influenced by the socialist ideas of fraternity and equality. All members of society can benefit from state ownership and participate in the running and organisation of the means of production.

Exam practice answers and quick quizzes at
www.hoddereducation.co.uk/myrevisionnotesdownloads

Marxism

Marxism is named after the most important key thinker within socialism: Karl Marx. Marxism argues the following:

- Humans are social beings whose natural state of fraternity, cooperation and selfishness has been perverted into **'a false consciousness'** by the greed, ruthlessness and selfishness inherent in capitalism.
- Social class is central to the perception of human history, which is described as a series of economic phases and contains two main classes. The capitalist stage sees the ruling class (bourgeoisie) take the surplus value of the workers (the proletariat), thereby 'exploiting', alienating and oppressing them.
- Marxism's main idea is **historical materialism**, in which economic conflict was the catalyst for historical and social development within society.
- Historical development was driven by a **dialectic**, a continuing chain of internal contradictions between two opposing forces, the exploited and the exploiters. History would pass through a series of stages, ending only with the withering away of the state and a perfect communist society, which would mark the end of history (see Table 3.1).
- Marx and Engels' ideas were adapted by numerous socialist thinkers during the twentieth century. Such thinkers are sometimes called post-Marxists or neo-Marxists.

Table 3.1 A summary of historical materialism and dialectic change (according to Marx and Engels)

1	Primitive societies with no economic organisation.
2	Slave-based societies — slaves are the main mode of production.
3	Feudal societies — land owned by the monarch is leased to lords, tenants and eventually serfs.
4	Emergence of capitalism.
5	Emergence of proletariat and **class consciousness**.
6	Revolution and destruction of capitalism.
7	Socialism (dictatorship of the proletariat).
8	Withering away of the socialist state.
9	**Communism** (end of history).

Class consciousness The moment when the proletariat would realise that capitalism was exploiting them, thus empowering them to begin the collective struggle of revolution, after which communism, the perfect socialist society, would be established.

Communism A society that is communally organised with an economy built on the elimination of private property in favour of common ownership, in which goods are held in common and available to all as needed.

Marxism An ideological and revolutionary theory of socialism that attempts to explain history scientifically in terms of the inevitable demise of capitalism and its replacement by communism. Marx was assisted in his writings by Engels, but he is often individually credited for this theory.

Historical materialism A theory that argues economic factors are the driving force for changing events. This economic case formed and shaped the superstructure, which was made up of culture, politics, law, religion, ideology and social consciousness.

Dialectic A clash of ideas and perceptions between each stage of history. It occurs when society's pre-existing set of values, as understood by the ruling class, is no longer valued by an alienated majority. A new society will be born from these two opposing forces.

Key thinker

Rosa Luxemburg (1871–1919)

Luxemburg was heavily influenced by the ideas of Marx and Engels, but her main contribution to socialism was to modify these ideas and to offer distinctive differences to the Marxism practised by Lenin and Trotsky in communist Russia.

The main ideas of Rosa Luxemburg were as follows:

- Evolutionary socialism was flawed as the economic capitalist system would be left intact and it would be impossible to reform the exploitation inherent within a capitalist society.
- Marx's historical materialism idea was flawed as capitalism did not need to reach a 'final stage' before it could be abolished. Like Lenin, Luxemburg argued that communist revolutions could happen in less economically developed societies than Marx and Engels had theorised.

- Lenin's belief in a 'vanguard elite' needed to guide the population towards revolution was also flawed. Class consciousness would develop 'spontaneously' as the proletariat struggled for workplace reforms and democracy. Mass strike action would help develop the revolutionary state.
- Luxemburg rejected Marx's 'dictatorship of the proletariat', arguing that after the revolution there should be free elections and a democracy built upon common ownership: **'Without general elections, without unrestricted freedom of the press and assembly, without a free struggle of opinion, life dies in every institution.'**
- Socialism must be internationalist rather than nationalist in nature, which was consistent with what Marx and Engels had argued.

Now test yourself

TESTED

2 Why does capitalism lead to exploitation?
3 What was Marx and Engels' materialist theory?
4 What did Marx and Engels mean by the 'dictatorship of the proletariat'?
5 What did Marx and Engels think communism was and what did they mean by the term 'the end of history'?
6 How did Rosa Luxemburg adapt the ideas of Marx and Engels?

Answers on p. 108

Evolutionary socialism

REVISED

An alternative to revolutionary socialism was evolutionary socialism, which is sometimes called **revisionist**. This sought to reform the worst excesses of capitalism by utilising the state to gradually reform society and the economy via democratic parliamentary institutions. The first type of revisionist socialism was called democratic socialism, which was popular from the late nineteenth century to the end of the Second World War. After the war, democratic socialism evolved into social democracy. In the late 1980s socialism revised itself again, with the Third Way.

Democratic socialism

- Democratic socialism argued for a socialist state via the ballot box rather than through revolution. The Fabian Society, led by Beatrice and Sidney Webb, believed that elite groups could be **'permeated'** by the moral supremacy of socialism over capitalism.
- Their ideas were hugely influential to the UK Labour Party and the Webbs helped write the party's constitution. Sidney wrote Clause 4, which asserted the common ownership of the means of production. The Fabian Society's ideas also influenced the German Social Democratic Party.

Revisionism This simply refers to reviewing and changing a political theory: for example, social democracy revised the ideas of democratic socialism. To differentiate between types of revisionism, the term 'neo-revisionism' is sometimes used. So the Third Way, a revision of social democracy, is sometimes called neo-revisionism.

Key thinker

Beatrice Webb (1858–1943)

Beatrice Webb was a member of the Fabian Society and believed that socialism would evolve peacefully through a combination of political action and education.

The main ideas of Beatrice Webb were as follows:
- **'The inevitability of gradualness'** was an evolutionary socialist belief that parliamentary democracy and not revolution would deliver the inevitable socialist society. It was inevitable because universal suffrage would lead to political equality as democracy would work in the interests of the working-class majority.
- Webb's ideas were therefore as fundamental as revolutionary socialism. However, she sought the overthrow of capitalism via the ballot box rather than through revolution.

- Webb argued that the working class would vote for socialist parties, which would begin to instigate social, economic and political reform, resulting in a socialist society.
- The expansion of the state was vital to deliver socialism as it would **'silently change its character...from police power to housekeeping on a national scale'**. The state would develop a highly trained elite of administrators and specialists to organise the socialist society.
- Equality of ownership, described in Clause 4 of the Labour Party constitution, would equate to extensive state nationalisation and not the workers taking direct control.
- Equality of ownership would involve high taxation of the wealthy so that the state could redistribute resources to the less well-off via an extensive welfare state.

Typical mistake

The process of 'gradualness' was not necessarily slow. Once reform began and the efficiency of socialism became clear, the state would transform 'to guide the mass of citizens to a socialist state' and would make steady progress.

Social democracy

Social democracy was the revisionism of democratic socialism and had its origins in Germany and the UK after the Second World War. Socialism faced hostility in the West as the Cold War unfolded and revisionist socialists had to deal with the reality that the post-war economic boom was increasing prosperity and living standards. Rather than alienating the working class, capitalism was delivering tangible benefits.
- Social democrats therefore argued that capitalism should be reformed and not replaced, which was a significant break with democratic socialism, which envisaged a fully socialist state.
- Social democracy attempted to utilise the wealth created by the free market by using state intervention to ensure that the proceeds were more fairly distributed across society. This would be done by:
  ○ supporting a mixed economy of both nationalised state industry and privately owned companies, which Attlee's Labour governments delivered between 1945 and 1951
  ○ economic state intervention, via Keynesian regulation of the economy, to ensure permanent full employment and growth
  ○ the welfare state, used to redistribute wealth and challenge poverty and social inequality.
- Following these reforms, Anthony Crosland argued that capitalism was no longer a system of oppression and that social justice was more important than common ownership.
- Crosland argued that social democracy must manage and maintain economic growth to pay for welfare spending, balancing economic efficiency and egalitarianism.

Key thinker

Anthony Crosland (1918–77)

Crosland was a Labour Party politician and Cabinet minister during the 1960s and 1970s. The ideas from his book, *The Future of Socialism* (1956), influenced social democracy in the UK.

The main ideas of Anthony Crosland were as follows:
- Crosland criticised the negative view of capitalist development, arguing that it did not drive social change and that **'the evolutionary and revolutionary philosophies of progress have proved false'**. The internal tensions required in Marx's dialectic of historical materialism were not present in post-war capitalism, in his opinion.

- Crosland concluded that **'Marx had little or nothing to offer the contemporary socialist'**.
- Rather, socialism was best served by **'state-managed capitalism'**. Crosland favoured a mixed economy that, rather than focusing on more public ownership, focused on equality of outcome facilitated by more spending on public services.
- Keynesian economics had made state-managed capitalism a reality and society could look forward to permanent economic growth and full employment. This would allow socialists to expand the welfare state and achieve social justice.
- Crosland's most famous attempt to ensure equality was to create comprehensive schools that would cater for all abilities and break down the social segregation of grammar schools.

Typical mistake

The term 'social democracy' was used by revolutionary socialists in the nineteenth century. However, students must be clear that its most commonly understood incarnation is as a revisionist form of socialism prevalent in Europe after the Second World War.

Exam tip

Remember that Crosland was a politician first and foremost, and practical politics stopped him from fully realising his ideas. Independent schools, which in many cases were far more segregated than grammar schools, remained exempt from his reforms as they were too politically difficult to abolish.

The Third Way

By the 1990s social democracy had also been revised and is commonly described as the Third Way, after the influential book by Anthony Giddens (it is also sometimes described as neo-revisionism). Giddens argued that developed economies have entered a post-Fordian period, with globalisation and mechanisation fragmenting traditional industrial production and atomising once tightly knit communities, alienating individuals. The Third Way was a response to these changes, incorporating neo-liberal ideas into existing social democratic ones to create a new branch of socialism.

The Third Way included the following ideas and principles:
- Giddens argued that the state must accept the free market and reject 'top-down' state intervention. An example in practice was New Labour utilising the private sector in the delivery of (what it perceived to be) better public services, via private finance initiatives and public–private partnerships.

Typical mistake

Revisionism does not replace the altered version of socialism. The Labour Party has MPs from all three branches of evolutionary socialism. The Third Way politics of New Labour have been in marked decline since 2010 and the party's current leader, Jeremy Corbyn, is an old-style social democrat.

- The role of the state therefore must move away from the economic and social engineering favoured by social democracy and embrace social investment in both infrastructure and education.
- There should be an emphasis on social inclusion and equality of opportunity, which would see everyone have the same chances in a meritocratic society. Marginalised groups were targeted by New Labour with tax credits, the minimum wage and educational maintenance grants.
- Traditional egalitarianism is scaled back — the Third Way did not endorse 'cradle to grave' policies of traditional social democracy. For example, in the UK there has been greater opportunity for young people to attend university, but they must contribute to their tuition costs.
- The Third Way promotion of education was also a social and economic investment. A more educated workforce would both improve an individual's life prospects and boost a market-orientated state's ability to compete globally.
- The Third Way social model downplays traditional socialist focuses on class differences and inequality, and endorses neo-liberal ideas such as championing the free market and self-reliance.
- More traditional socialist ideas such as redistribution of wealth are far less prominent than in social democracy.

Exam tip

Blair's Labour Party rarely used the term 'Third Way', preferring to rebrand itself 'New Labour' (although the party was still officially called the Labour Party). Terms such as the Third Way and neo-revisionism are used more by academics. Students should use the term favoured by the examination specification: the Third Way.

Key thinker

Anthony Giddens (1938–)

Giddens is a sociologist whose political ideas have offered a neo-revisionist form of socialism, espousing a Third Way between neo-liberalism and traditional social democracy, that has influenced not just New Labour but reformist socialist parties in all advanced industrialised democracies.

The main ideas of Anthony Giddens are as follows:
- Free-market capitalism enriches and empowers society and, alongside capitalism and individualism, is irreversible. Socialism must harness the benefits of the free market while neutralising its corrosive effects upon community and fraternity.
- Therefore there must be a reconciliation to marry neo-liberal ideas of economic empowerment with the cohesion of social democracy's view of society. This accepts individualism but stresses that individuals live, work and thrive in a community of interdependence and reciprocity.

- Individuals would therefore become stakeholders and have both rights and responsibilities within society.
- This revisionism would reimagine the role of the state within the economy and society.
- First, it involves an abandonment of state intervention and the state-managed social democracy espoused by Anthony Crosland based on the economic ideas of John Maynard Keynes, as free-market economic ideas are broadly accepted.
- Second, it advocates an abandonment of the economic and social engineering of social democracy espoused by Crosland. Revisionist socialism should prioritise infrastructure such as community services and public transport while focusing on equality of opportunity, particularly in education.
- Greater equality of opportunity would be provided by using free-market wealth to fund infrastructure and public services. Social inclusiveness would provide wider opportunities for the disadvantaged, e.g. increased access to higher education, replacing comprehensives with academy schools.

Revision activity

Briefly distinguish between these forms of liberalism:
- revolutionary socialism
- democratic socialism
- social democracy
- the Third Way.

Tensions within socialism

REVISED

The following are the main tensions that exist among different strands of socialist thought. In each case they are linked to one of the four key themes of human nature, society, the state and the economy.

Human nature

- Socialists believe humans are cooperative and altruistic but that human nature is not fixed but moulded by society.
- Revolutionary socialists and social democrats argue that capitalism has distorted human nature into a 'false consciousness' of greed and selfishness.
- The Third Way argues that capitalism can be beneficial to human nature. Economic rewards can be utilised for the common good if correctly married to core socialist beliefs of cooperation, fraternity and community.

Society

- Socialists broadly agree that society must respond to the negative effects of capitalism and be remodelled. However, they disagree on the methods of instigating this change and what the core principles of a socialist society should be.
- Revolutionary socialists such as Marx and Engels, and those directly influenced by their ideas such as Luxemburg, argue that the ideas and values of capitalism have infected society to such an extent that revolution is the only alternative.
- Democratic socialists such as Beatrice Webb and social democrats like Anthony Crosland argue that society can be gradually reformed in the interests of social justice, via parliamentary government, which will humanise capitalism.
- Democratic socialists such as Webb argue that reform will lead to a socialist society (achieved gradually without a revolution), whereas social democrats and the Third Way argue for a humanising of capitalism that would be dismissed by Marx and Engels as well as Luxemburg and Webb as being impossible due to capitalism's exploitative nature.
- The Third Way argues for a positive role for individualism and the free market. Giddens states that the selfish aspects of neo-liberalism could be negated if married to social democratic principles of community and fraternity. All other branches of socialism find it difficult to reconcile the neo-liberal aspects of the Third Way with their distinctive branch of socialism.

The state

Socialists have different visions for the role of the state:

- Revolutionary socialists like Marx and Engels argued that after revolution the state would wither away to produce stateless communism. Revolutionary socialists like Luxemburg disagree and argue that the capitalist state should be replaced by a socialist state complete with democratic elections and free speech.
- Democratic socialists and social democrats argue that the state can remodel society without a revolution in an evolutionary fashion, with Webb and Crosland both arguing that parliamentary democracy can gradually instigate socialist reform.
- The Third Way argues that the state should support the free market so that it can improve society and also should decentralise political power and allow the private sector to run public services. No other branch of socialism has such a positive role for the free market.
- Neo-Marxists like Ralph Miliband argued that democratic socialist and social democrat governments had struggled to implement their socialist agendas as the state's elite — the civil service, the judiciary, the armed forces and big business — frustrated socialist reforms.
- Miliband agreed with Marx and Engels that the 'parliamentary road' to socialism was flawed and socialism could be achieved only via a revolution.

The economy

- Marx, Engels and Luxemburg all viewed the free market and private property as incompatible with socialism's core principles and argued for revolution (and in differing ways) a remodelling of the economy along socialist lines.
- Democratic socialists such as Beatrice Webb agree with this assessment but argue that a socialist state will be achieved not by revolution but gradually via reform.
- Neither social democrats nor the Third Way envisage a fully socialist state such as the one envisaged by revolutionary socialists or democratic socialists.
- Social democrats such as Crosland argue for a mixed economy rather than increasing public ownership. A state-managed economy would adopt Keynesian economics to ensure permanent economic growth and full employment, and the proceeds of the economy would be spent on expanding the welfare state.
- The Third Way argues for the abandonment of state-managed Keynesian economics and instead supports neo-liberal economics that accepts the privatisation of formerly nationalised utilities. The greater revenues generated from this style of economic management could then fund public spending that could be focused on equality of opportunity.

Now test yourself

TESTED

7 Suggest three ways in which socialists promote collectivism.
8 Why do some socialists prefer revolution to reform?
9 Why did Marx and Engels see social class as such an important central concept?
10 Why did Luxemburg combine revolution and democracy in her ideas?
11 Why did Webb see the role of the state as crucial to her ideas?
12 What did Crosland mean by state-managed capitalism?
13 Why did Giddens argue against state-managed capitalism?

Answers on pp. 108–9

Revision activity

1 How do the different socialist traditions differ in understanding:
  - the state
  - the economy?
2 Identify the key term associated with socialism which is described in each of these cases:
  (a) Property that is no longer owned by an individual but by the collective.
  (b) A theory of history that attempts to scientifically explain why capitalism will be replaced by communism.
  (c) A theory of economics where the government manages the economy and delivers economic growth and full employment.
  (d) Comradeship between human beings.
  (e) Individuals working collaboratively.
  (f) A free-market economic system with the central tenets of private property and competition between individuals and companies.
  (g) A communal economy based on the common ownership of wealth and a cooperative social existence.
  (h) A redefining of socialism which involves a less radical view of socialism's relationship with capitalism.
  (i) A group of individuals hitherto ignorant, suddenly realising that they are being exploited.
  (j) The Marxist theory that the economic base informs the superstructure.
  (k) Distributing wealth so that it limits inequality and is morally acceptable.
  (l) Historical development is caused by internal contradictions that develop within society.

Exam practice

You must use appropriate thinkers you have studied to support your answer and consider both sides in a balanced way.
1 To what extent is socialism committed to collectivism? [24]
2 To what extent is socialism committed to equality? [24]
3 To what extent do socialists disagree about the economy? [24]

Answers and quick quiz 3 online

ONLINE

Summary

You should now have an understanding of:
- the fact that socialists view human nature as malleable and defined for good or ill by society
- why revolutionary socialists like Marx and Engels thought it inevitable that capitalism would be replaced by communism
- why Marx/Engels and Luxemburg thought revolutionary socialism was the only way to achieve communism and why they rejected evolutionary socialism

- why Marx and Engels would have been surprised and revolted by the communist societies that were inspired by their ideas
- the development of evolutionary socialism from democratic socialism to social democracy to the Third Way and how its attitudes change towards society, the state and the economy
- the contribution of at least the five key thinkers to the development of socialist thought (remember that Marx and Engels count as one key thinker).

4 Feminism

The origins of feminism

- Feminist role models and themes have been traced back to ancient Greece. However, as a set of political ideas it is argued that the movement has come in four waves from 1790 to the present day (see Table 4.1).
- **Patriarchy** is a common theme for explaining female oppression, but feminism cannot be described as a coherent political idea as there is disagreement and debate over the exact role and nature of patriarchy as well as potential solutions to female inequality.
- Liberal feminists wish to reform society of its patriarchal elements.
- Socialist and radical feminists believe society is beyond reform and argue for revolution to transform society (although they differ on the exact format of the revolution).
- Some aspects of radical feminism from the 1970s are now almost historical relics. The idea of women living in separate lesbian societies, for example, is not a solution favoured by many modern feminists.
- Liberal feminism has seen success in western democracies with legislation granting equal rights across a broad spectrum of society since the 1960s. However, in other parts of the world, patriarchy and the oppression of women remain largely unaltered.
- Consequently, fourth wave post-modern feminists argue that there is more to understanding the female experience than mere gender and that women have multiple identities and circumstances (including class, race, demographic, religion, social media, etc.).
- Today, third and fourth wave feminists argue that patriarchy is constantly mutating and women face new complex forms of oppression that are not just limited to male oppression and that vary dramatically depending upon a woman's particular circumstances.

> **Patriarchy** Feminists use this term to describe society dominated by men and where women's status is inferior. Patriarchy can be so powerful that women are unaware that it is actually happening.

Feminism has developed over four key stages. Table 4.1 places different branches of feminism, feminist thinkers and ideas into chronological order. The key thinkers are in bold.

Core ideas of feminism
Human nature

REVISED

- The two main issues of human nature that concern feminists are the conceptualisations of sex and gender.
- Sex refers to biological differences between men and women. Gender is used to explain innate characteristics, such as men being logical and women being sensitive and caring.
- While biological differences are undeniable, feminists argue that gender characteristics are not innate but are imposed upon women by a patriarchal society.
- Gender roles are artificially constructed by patriarchy and create societal norms. Simone de Beauvoir argues that these gender differences are created by men and are not natural.
- Sheila Rowbotham, a socialist feminist, argues that women's consciousness is created by men as part of the capitalist machine.

Table 4.1 Key political thinkers and their ideas

First wave (1790–1940s)	Second wave feminism (1960s–1980s)	Third wave feminism (1990s to early 2000s)	Fourth wave feminism (post-2008)
Liberal feminism	**Liberal feminism**	**Post-feminism**	**Post-modern feminism**
Mary Wollstonecroft *(rights for women)*	Betty Friedan[1] *(personhood)*	Camille Paglia *(against 'victimhood')*	Femen *(sexual exploitation, dictatorship, religion)*
Charlotte Perkins Gilman *(sex and domestic economics, societal pressure)*	**Socialist feminism (revolutionary)**	**Liberal feminism**	SlutWalk *(rape)*
Suffragists *(emancipation)*	**Sheila Rowbotham (capitalism and family)**	Sylvia Walby *(six structures of patriarchy)*	Pussy Riot *(religion, dictatorship, LGBT)*
	Juliet Mitchell *(capitalism and family life)*	Naomi Wolf *(body image, technology, pornography)*	Kira Cochrane *(technology)*
			Kimberlé Crenshaw ***(intersectionality)***
Simone de Beauvoir *(sex and gender, otherness)*	**Socialist feminism** *(reformist)*	**Post-modern feminism**	
Socialist feminism	Chicago Women's Liberation Front	Jennifer Baumgardner and Amy Richards *(successive generational reinterpretation of feminism)*	
Friedrich Engels[2] *(revolutionary, communism)*	**Radical feminism**	Natasha Walter *(political, economic, social and 'hypersexualisation')*	
Radical feminism	Carol Hanisch *(personal is political)*		
Suffragettes	**Kate Millett (family, art and literature)**		
	Shulamith Firestone *(reproduction)*		
	Andrea Dworkin *(pornography)*		
	Germaine Greer *(sexuality)*		
	Charlotte Bunch *(separate societies, lesbianism as a political choice)*		
	Ecofeminism		
	Carolyn Merchant[3] *(patriarchy dominates nature and women)*		
	Difference feminism		
	Carol Gilligan *(different not equal)*		
	Post-modern feminism		
	bell hooks *(women of colour)*		

1 For more details on Betty Friedan, see chapter 1, page 14.

2 For more details on Friedrich Engels, see chapter 1, page 33.

3 For more details on Carolyn Merchant, see chapter 8, page 104.

Exam practice answers and quick quizzes at
www.hoddereducation.co.uk/myrevisionnotesdownloads

Key thinker

Simone de Beauvoir (1908–96)

De Beauvoir, an early French feminist, was known as the first existential feminist.

The main ideas of Simone de Beauvoir were as follows:

- As an existentialist feminist, de Beauvoir argued for individual freedom above the societal conventions and constrictions placed on women.
- Sex versus gender: the biological differences of sex have been used as a justification for predetermining the role of a 'woman' by a process of socialisation by a male-dominated state and society: **'One is not born, but rather becomes a woman.'** De Beauvoir therefore rejected the existence of 'a woman's nature'. All roles within society should be gender neutral.
- De Beauvoir rejected the concept of 'motherhood' and the idea that women were predetermined with a nurturing instinct. Socialisation by parents, education and society removes women's freedom to choose as they are indoctrinated from birth to roles and behaviours determined by men.
- She developed the idea of **otherness**, whereby men have characterised themselves as 'the norm' and have designated women as different.
- 'Otherness' has been imposed on women by men. Women have internalised this false sense of natural inferiority and will need to become conscious of their socialisation and indoctrination if they are to contest the roles that they have been designated.
- Women need to liberate themselves and seek freedom from oppression to find their individual identity. Gender roles for family and workplace must be equal, the state must fund childcare, and there should be widespread contraception and legalisation of abortion to allow women control of their bodies.
- This will involve equality of opportunity in gender roles, sexual liberation via state-funded abortion and contraception, and freedom from the set parameters of the nuclear family, via state-funded childcare.

- Betty Friedan argues that the patriarchal cultural attitudes were so powerful and persuasive that women and men thought of them as normal and natural rather than artificially constructed.
- Post-modern feminists such as bell hooks argue that women have multiple identities that are not based on gender alone and therefore face multiple sources of oppression such as racism or class exploitation.
- Most feminists argue that the general status of women in society should not be affected by their biological status and that gender differences are artificially constructed by society. Liberal, radical, socialist and post-modern feminists disagree on many points but are all **equality feminists**, believing that biological differences are inconsequential and gender differences artificial.
- However, a minority of feminists, **difference feminists**, disagree with equality feminism and believe in **essentialism**, arguing that biological differences are consequential as they determine gender differences, which are not constructed by society.
- Difference feminists argue that men and women are fundamentally different and women must embrace their distinctiveness.
- Difference feminists also argue that women's inferior status can be explained by biological sexual differences, which have been used as a justification for determining gender roles within society.

Otherness Women are treated as an inferior minority who are subordinate to men in a patriarchal society.

Equality feminism Argues for an elimination of cultural differences between the genders and a pursuit of absolute equality. Liberal, radical, socialist and post-modern feminists all have different visions of how this will be achieved.

Difference feminists Perceive women as biologically and culturally different. They argue that these differences need to be recognised and celebrated.

Essentialism The idea that biological factors determine the different characters and behaviours of men and women so that certain behaviours are 'natural' and not socially constructed.

Exam tip

Be clear that most feminists are equality feminists, and difference feminists have been criticised within the feminist movement for undermining feminist goals by arguing that women have an innate biological predetermination to be more passive, nurturing and caring than men.

- Difference feminists like Carol Gilligan argue that equality feminism has the unintended consequence of encouraging women to replicate male behaviour, alienating women from their own gender distinctiveness.
- **Cultural feminism**, a more extreme version of difference feminism, challenges the dominance of male values in society and argues that 'women's values' should be promoted, as they are superior.

> **Cultural feminism** Very similar to difference feminism as it argues that women are born with different cultural characteristics as well as biological ones. Women are more caring and nurturing than men, who are more competitive and aggressive.

Now test yourself

TESTED

1 Why is the distinction between sex and gender so important within feminism?

Answer on p. 109

Society

REVISED

Core ideas include the following:

- Patriarchy is pervasive and is present in every facet of society: religion, culture, education, media, sports, politics. Patriarchy has been consciously constructed by men to oppress women and to designate them a gender role.
- Sylvia Walby identifies six overlapping structures that take different forms in society at various times:
  - ○ **State:** historically the state under-represents women in power. The few in positions of power are hindered by **discrimination** in a male sexist culture with anti-family working hours.
  - ○ **Household:** society conditions women to believe their natural role is as mother/homemaker.
  - ○ **Violence:** many women suffer physical violence at the hands of men (one in four women will experience domestic violence).
  - ○ **Paid work:** when women do have jobs they find themselves in low-paid/part-time roles, often assisting men. Women-centric careers tend to be linked to **gender stereotypes** of nurturing, such as nursing or teaching children.
  - ○ **Sexuality:** women are made to feel that their sexual feelings are abnormal, wrong and deviant.
  - ○ **Culture:** society reinforces its roles on women, from the woman being the primary carer through to objectifying how women should look.
- Liberal feminists argue that patriarchal society can be reformed via state and cultural action.
- Socialist feminists argue that society is economically determined by male capitalists.
- Radical feminists argue that patriarchal society is too pervasive to be reformed and there needs to be a revolutionary change in the discourse between men and women.
- Post-modern feminists argue that society is too multifaceted to be determined by one variable such as gender.

> **Discrimination** Treating a group or an individual less favourably than another group or individual. In this case, it refers to women being treated less favourably than men in a variety of ways.
>
> **Gender stereotype** The argument that men's and women's gender roles are predetermined by society so that they are socialised to behave in a certain way.

Exam tip

When distinguishing between sex and gender you should emphasise that feminists argue that gender roles are socially constructed, which means that they are changeable. This means that gender inequality is not natural or inevitable.

The state

Core ideas include the following:
- Unlike liberals, conservatives and socialists, feminists lack a distinctive theory of the state and they restrict themselves to perceiving the state as the vessel through which patriarchy is reinforced within society.
- Socialist and radical feminists argue that patriarchal culture is so embedded in society and the state that it is fanciful to imagine that the state can combat patriarchy.
- Liberal feminists agree that the state has been an instrument to reinforce patriarchy but argue that this function can change and that the state can be a conduit for reform and tackling patriarchy.
- Post-modern feminists argue that there is a complexity to state oppression that other branches of feminism miss because of their tendency to generalise. bell hooks argues that race is as important as gender, for example.

The economy

Core ideas include the following:
- Feminists are united in their belief that the economic world discriminates against women.
- Discrimination includes unpaid labour in the home and a lack of **equality of opportunity** in the workplace.
- Friedrich Engels argued that women are often reduced to being a **reserve army of labour**.
- Some socialist feminists maintain that a revolution to overthrow capitalism is needed for true equality in society. Sheila Rowbotham argues that women must become a political force to facilitate this communist process.
- Post-modern feminist bell hooks argues that race and class can be as important as gender in understanding economic oppression. Black women from poor backgrounds face poverty and inequalities that middle-class women will not experience.

> **Equality of opportunity** Everyone, irrespective of their gender, should have the same life chances within society.
>
> **Reserve army of labour** The idea that women constitute a spare workforce that can be called on as and when needed.

Different types of feminism

Liberal feminism

Liberal feminism is **reformist** and argues that, via democratic pressure, gender stereotypes can be eliminated. Unlike radical feminism and socialist feminism, liberal feminists do not believe that there needs to a revolutionary change in the way society, the state or the economy is organised. Liberal feminists focus on the public sphere (society) rather than the private sphere (family).

Some key ideas of liberal feminists include the following:
- They are heavily influenced by liberal values of individualism and foundational equality. Women require the same liberty as men in determining their role within society, both as wives/mothers and within the labour force.
- First wave feminists like Mary Wollstonecraft argued for **political equality** and that women should have the vote. The assumption was that political emancipation would lead to **gender equality**.

> **Reformist** Believing that society can be reformed. In a feminist context, this means that negative consequences of oppression can, by legislation, gradually alter until equality is achieved.
>
> **Political equality** Women should have the same right to vote and protest as men.
>
> **Gender equality** Men and women should be treated the same within society.

- Women should have the same **legal equality**, particularly in relation to the economic sphere of property ownership.
- First wave feminists such as Charlotte Perkins Gilman were among the first to argue that biological differences were irrelevant and that women were intellectually equal to men.
- Betty Friedan argued that society confined women to the narrow roles of housewife and mother, which alienated and oppressed women. She championed equality of opportunity across the public sphere.
- Third wave liberal feminists argue that patriarchy is constantly changing and adapting in the ways that it oppresses women. Naomi Wolf claimed that patriarchy and technology determine how women perceive beauty. Photoshopped images of women portray an unobtainable fantasy image that oppresses young women.
- Liberal feminists are reformist and disagree with radical feminists over the omnipresence of patriarchy. Liberal feminists believe it is possible for discrimination and oppression to be reformed in both state and society.

> **Legal equality** Everybody should be treated the same in the eyes of the law. For feminists this means that women should have exactly the same lawful rights as men.

Typical mistake

Students sometimes argue that conservatives are unsympathetic to feminist ideas because they value tradition. However, reformist branches of conservatism such as one-nation conservatism and that Christian democracy have embraced the idea of 'changing to conserve' and are sympathetic to liberal feminism. Neo-liberals' core beliefs mean that they too embrace liberal feminism.

Exam tip

Remember the crossover link with liberalism. Foundational equality refers to rights that all humans have by virtue of being born and that should not be taken away. Mary Wollstonecraft is a key thinker within liberalism who argued for formal equality, which would give women the same legal and political rights as men.

Key thinker

Charlotte Perkins Gilman (1860–1935)

Gilman expressed her version of early feminism in both fictional works and scholarly writings.

The main ideas of Charlotte Perkins Gilman were as follows:

- Gilman reacted against social Darwinism, which argued that male domination of society was linked to Darwin's idea of survival of the fittest. She asserted that biological differences were irrelevant in a modern society and that women were intellectually equal to men, which is what matters most in modern society.
- Sex and domestic economics were interlinked. Women were reliant on their sexual assets to gratify their husbands, who in turn would support the family financially.
- Societal pressure forced young girls to conform to motherhood and the domestic role with toys and clothes conforming to gender stereotype. Gilman argued for gender-neutral toys and clothes to counter this.
- Only economic independence could give women freedom and equality with men.
- Motherhood should not prevent women from working outside the home.
- The traditional role of women in the nuclear family with sole responsibility for childcare and domesticity was comparable to slavery. Gilman argued for a communal form of living whereby child rearing and housework would be shared, allowing women a wider role in society.

Typical mistake

Darwin's *On the Origin of Species* (1859) was concerned solely with evolution of the human species and the natural selection of plants and animals. Social Darwinists appropriated Darwin's ideas and applied them to human beings. A common mistake that students make is that Gilman was rebutting Darwin's ideas.

Exam practice answers and quick quizzes at
www.hoddereducation.co.uk/myrevisionnotesdownloads

Socialist feminism

All socialist feminists argue that economics leads to gender equality and that capitalism causes patriarchy. However, socialist feminism cannot be described as coherent as there are different branches, revolutionary and reformist, and each has differing solutions and disagreements.

Revolutionary socialist feminism

- Friedrich Engels was the first to argue that economics caused gender inequality and capitalism created patriarchy.
- Engels argued that capitalism altered pre-existing societal structures, which meant that women were needed as unpaid helpers to enable male workers to be employed in the workplace.
- He claimed that women were complicit in both reproducing the workforce and socialising their children in the continuing cycle of capitalistic oppression.
- He suggested that women were also a reserve army of labour, to be cast off when they were no longer needed.
- He argued that women had always been economically oppressed because they had been deprived of property ownership.
- Building on Engels' ideas, Gilman argued that the first part of female emancipation was economic independence.
- Rowbotham adopted a Marxist theory of history, concluding that women have always been oppressed and that a revolution was needed to destroy capitalism and patriarchy.
- Juliet Mitchell criticises Engels' belief that women's oppression results wholly from capitalism. She argues that aspects of patriarchy are unconnected to capitalism and that it is necessary to fight capitalism and patriarchy as distinct entities to achieve a classless society.

Key thinker

Sheila Rowbotham (1943–)

For Sheila Rowbotham, female oppression has economic roots, but also stems from the traditional nuclear family and the cultural dominance of male sexuality. Her main ideas are as follows:

- Adapting Marxist historical materialism, Rowbotham concluded that women have always been oppressed. Marriage is like feudalism, with a woman akin to a serf paying feudal dues to her husband.
- Capitalism worsened this oppression and women were doubly oppressed: forced to sell their labour to survive in the workplace and to cede their labour in the family home.
- Alienation from both capitalism and patriarchy meant a **'revolution within a revolution'** was needed to restructure both sources of oppression.
- Men do not fully understand the nature of oppression of women: **'Men will often admit other women are oppressed but not you.'**
- The family performs a dual function: to subject and discipline women to the demands of capitalism and to offer a place of refuge for men from the alienation of capitalism.

Reformist socialist feminism

- Socialist feminists influenced by democratic socialism argue for state ownership of industry as this would eliminate discrimination in the workplace.
- Socialist feminists influenced by social democracy, such as the Chicago Women's Liberation Front, pre-empted post-modern feminism by calling for reforms that would benefit working-class women and for the use of education to change patriarchal culture in the workplace.

Now test yourself

2 What are the differences between liberal and socialist feminists?

Answer on p. 109

TESTED

Radical feminism

Radical feminism's origins lie with second wave feminism. All radical feminists argue that society is purely patriarchal and is a system of oppression unconnected with any other ideology. Radical feminists argue for fundamental changes to society's structure. However, radical feminism cannot be described as coherent as there are different branches with different causes and solutions to patriarchy that are often in conflict with each other.

- Liberal feminists mostly focus on the public sphere of society when discussing their ideas. Second wave radical feminists argued that both the **public sphere** and the **private sphere** of life must be addressed and claimed 'the personal is political'.
- Radical feminists argue that patriarchy is prevalent in the private sphere of life such as the family. Traditionally, liberal feminists and politicians do not focus on this personal sphere.
- By ignoring the private aspect of women's life, radical feminists argue that the oppression of women's domestic circumstance is ignored. Personal life has to be political if patriarchal oppression is to be challenged.
- Difference feminists argue that a world dominated by feminine essence would be more peaceful and environmentally friendly. Difference feminists have influenced ecofeminists, who see both the oppression of women and the oppression of nature as an aspect of the male need to dominate. Naturally nurturing, women are therefore better suited to co-exist and protect the environment.

Public sphere The visible area of society where relationships are public, such as the workplace, within culture and civic life.

Private sphere The area of society where relationships are seen as private. These relationships are less visible and centred on the home and domestic life.

Now test yourself

3 What is meant by 'the personal is political'?
4 Contrast the ideas of equality and difference feminists.

Answers on p. 109

TESTED

Typical mistake

Beware of broad generalisations. Students sometimes argue that difference feminists want female supremacy and matriarchy, which is a simplification. Rather, they promote the equality and sometimes superiority of female characteristics and argue for these to be recognised.

Focus on different aspects of patriarchy

- Kate Millett argued that the family both oppressed the mother and socialised children into rigid gender roles. The practice of dropping one's surname demonstrates a loss of identity. She also argued patriarchy was reflected in the degrading treatment of women in art and literature.
- Erin Pizzey's analysis of 'the personal is political' focused on domestic violence within family life.
- Charlotte Bunch argued that heterosexual relationships were based on power and that lesbianism was a political choice.
- Germaine Greer argued that patriarchy had socialised women to view their sexual desires as unfeminine and to be embarrassed about their bodies. Women had been indoctrinated to believe they must try to retain eternal youth rather than physically and emotionally embrace their age and experience.
- Andrea Dworkin argued that pornography was symptomatic of men's perception of women as sex objects.
- Shulamith Firestone (adopting Marx and Engels) saw history as a dialectic struggle over gender relating to biological differences between men and women. Patriarchy has always existed as women have always been enslaved by men.

Key thinker

Kate Millett (1934–2017)

Millett believed the state is merely the agent of patriarchy. It is part of the problem but not the solution.

The main ideas of Kate Millett were as follows:
- The family was the chief institution, reinforcing patriarchy. Dismantling the traditional family unit was the key to a sexual revolution.
- Patriarchy granted men ownership over their wife and children, which entrenched sexism, the idea of male superiority. Marriage saw women lose their identity by having to take their husband's surname and offer domestic service and sexual consent in return for being financially supported.

- The family unit was the chief instigator of socialising the young and supporting masculine authority in all aspects of society, while women were largely marginalised.
- The portrayal of women in art and literature reinforces patriarchy. Millett argues that sex in culture subjugates women. Women are also portrayed as possessions of men, to be fought over and owned.
- Millett is critical of romantic love, monogamous marriage and the family unit as this trinity reinforced patriarchy. A sexual revolution was needed to destroy patriarchy.
- Patriarchy also reinforced heterosexualism as being superior to bisexual or homosexual relationships.

Different solutions to patriarchy

- The nuclear family should be abolished and replaced by communal living and child rearing (Kate Millett).
- The nuclear family should be abolished and replaced by lesbian communities (Andrea Dworkin and Charlotte Bunch).
- Germaine Greer argued for sexual liberation and the abandonment of traditional marriage and the male domination that this entails. She favoured communal living and child rearing.
- Firestone's perfect society would eliminate gender distinctions and embrace androgyny (the physical characteristics of both sexes). She envisaged a world where women would be able to procreate without men.
- Difference feminism focuses on gender differences and even the superiority of women, via its cultural feminist branch. Women must accept and promote their female qualities.

Exam tip

Be sure to acknowledge the similarities between some branches of radical feminism and revolutionary socialism. Radical feminists substitute 'patriarchy' in the place of 'capitalism' as the explanation for why the exploited members of society are women rather than workers.

Now test yourself

TESTED

5 What are the differences between liberal and radical feminism?
6 What are the differences between socialist and radical feminism?

Answers on p. 109

Post-feminist critique of liberal feminism and radical feminism

REVISED

Post-feminists writing in the late 1980s and early 1990s argued that most of the feminist goals had been achieved and that women should move on. Writers such as Camille Paglia criticised feminism for portraying women as 'victims' and argued that women needed to take responsibility for their own life and sexual conduct. Post-feminism has been roundly criticised for examining feminism solely through a white, middle-class framework that ignores the complexity of female experience that post-modern feminism explores.

Typical mistake

Students often confuse post-feminism with post-modern feminism, which can be disastrous as they are two different things. Be clear that you know the difference.

Post-modern feminism

Post-modern feminism rejects the broad generalisations inherent in other feminist traditions as being overly simplistic. Gender is not the only variable affecting women; there are numerous other interacting factors — race, class, religion, age, country of origin, to name but a few. Post-modern feminism embraces the complexity of reality and therefore has a diverse set of definitions for 'feminism' and 'patriarchy', given the multiple identities that women possess.

Themes of post-modern feminism

- Intersectionality challenged the notion that gender is the most important factor in understanding women's lives. bell hooks first argued that race was as important as gender in understanding oppression of black women; in the USA in the early 1980s. The term 'intersectionality' was coined later by Kimberlé Crenshaw to help conceptualise overlapping oppression.
- hooks was critical of second wave feminists excluding minority groups such as 'women of colour'. Feminism, hooks argued, was dominated by the voices and concerns of white, middle-class women.

> **Exam tip**
>
> If faced with a question that involves discussing the various branches of feminism, be explicit about which branch you are discussing. You must also explain why the different branches of feminism disagree with each other. Make sure you use all of the key feminist thinkers before discussing other feminists.

Key thinker

bell hooks (1952–)

hooks believes society is full of complex relationships between different minorities.

The main ideas of bell hooks are as follows:
- hooks argues that children are socialised into gender stereotypes from a young age.
- She broadened the feminist debate as she felt it was too focused on middle- and upper-class, college-educated white women. hooks focused on **'women of colour'** and all social classes.
- 'Women of colour' faced both racial discrimination and sexual discrimination

and neither the civil rights movement nor the women's movement recognised this dual problem.
- There is a need to reach out to women neglected by mainstream feminist thought, such as women of different ethnicities and socio-economic classes.
- hooks' ideas greatly influenced the idea of **intersectionality** — coined by Kimberlé Crenshaw — which challenged the feminist assumption that gender was the most important factor in determining a woman's life experiences.

Intersectionality Challenging the belief that gender is the singular most important factor in determining a woman's experience. Rather, women have multiple overlapping intersecting identities, including race, class, age and religion. Generalising about the female experiences of patriarchy is pointless when white middle-class women will have a very different experience from black working-class women and other 'types' of women.

> **Typical mistake**
>
> bell hooks' decision to spell her name without capital letters is a political statement to distance herself from the ego associated with names. However, so ingrained is the habit of using capital letters when writing names that students constantly render bell hooks's name incorrectly.

- hooks argued for the need to recognise a plethora of female experiences to construct a genuine, inclusive 'sisterhood'.
- Natasha Walker, writing in 1999, echoed hooks in arguing for a more complex assessment of inequality among women across political, economic and social aspects of life. In 2010 she argued that modern women are now facing new pressures of 'hypersexualisation'.
- Jennifer Baumgardner and Amy Richards embraced post-modernism in their *Manifesta* (2000), which argued that successive generations of

Exam practice answers and quick quizzes at
www.hoddereducation.co.uk/myrevisionnotesdownloads

women would need to establish and construct what feminism meant to them.

- Post-modern feminists such as Femen (an organisation founded in the Ukraine) perceive nudity as empowering and have made topless protests against important aspects of patriarchy: sexual exploitation, dictatorship and religion.
- SlutWalk is a global movement of post-modern feminists who dress like 'sluts' for protest marches after a police officer argued that 'women should avoid dressing like sluts'. This was a patriarchal attitude that partially excused rape by stating a women's appearance could be a mitigating factor.
- Fourth wave post-modern feminists like Kira Cochrane argue that technology is a source of misogyny and patriarchy via social media.
- Conversely, Cochrane argues that technology can be used to 'call out' and challenge sexism and misogyny in the public sphere.

Now test yourself

7 What is the difference between post-feminism and post-modern feminism?
8 Why is post-modern feminism critical of the other branches of feminism?

Answers on p. 109

TESTED ☐

> ### Revision activity
>
> How do the different branches of feminism differ in their understanding of:
> - human nature
> - society
> - the state
> - the economy?

Now test yourself

TESTED ☐

9 Identify the key term associated with feminism which is described in each of these cases:
   (a) All individuals should be treated the same in the eyes of the law.
   (b) Women are biologically and culturally dissimilar.
   (c) Challenging the belief that gender is the most important factor in a woman's experience.
   (d) A society dominated by men.
   (e) A broad branch of feminism which argues that cultural differences between genders should be eliminated.
   (f) Treating a group or individual less favourably.
   (g) The idea that gender roles are predetermined by society.
   (h) Women are a spare workforce.
   (i) A belief that society can be successfully modified.
   (j) The visible area of society.
   (k) Women are treated as an inferior minority, different from and subordinate to men.
   (l) All individuals should have the same life chances.
   (m) Biological factors determine different characteristics which are 'natural'.
   (n) Women should be allowed the same rights to vote and protest as men.
   (o) Women have distinct cultural characteristics.
   (p) The often invisible area of society.
   (q) Men and women should be treated the same within society.

Answers on p. 110

> ### Revision activity
>
> How do the following branches of feminism understand the concept of patriarchy?
> - Liberal feminism.
> - Socialist feminism.
> - Radical feminism.
> - Post-modern feminism.

Now test yourself

10 Identify a key feminist thinker associated with these ideas:
   (a) Women are oppressed economically and culturally.
   (b) Gender stereotyping.
   (c) Otherness.
   (d) Family as a source of patriarchy.
   (e) Mainstream feminism excludes women of colour.

Answers on p. 110

Exam practice

You must use appropriate thinkers you have studied to support your answer and consider both sides in a balanced way.

1 To what extent do feminists agree on sex and gender?   [24]
2 To what extent do feminists agree over the concept of patriarchy?   [24]
3 To what extent do feminists agree that the personal is political?   [24]

Answers and quick quiz 4 online

ONLINE

Summary

You should now have an understanding of:
- the distinction between liberal, social, radical and post-modern feminism and be aware of the various internal differences within these branches of feminism (essays asking you to discuss diverse branches of feminist thought require you to explain why they strongly oppose each other rather than just discussing the differences)
- how liberal feminism can be explained by the core liberal doctrine of rationalism; likewise, how socialist feminism can be understood by the core socialist doctrine of collectivism
- how the different feminist branches are often reactions to each other:

   – socialist feminism and radical feminism are both reactions to, and critiques of, liberal feminism
   – post-modern feminism is a critique of the broad generalisation inherent in earlier feminist thought

   (Table 4.1 will help you track the development of each branch)
- the fact that the majority of feminism is sympathetic to equality feminism, while difference feminism and its sub-strand, cultural feminism, is very much a minority position within feminist thought
- the contribution of at least the five key thinkers to the development of feminist thought.

5 Anarchism

The origins of anarchism

Anarchism is a term given to a collection of ideas and political movements which have in common a belief that the state should be abolished either because it is evil and exploitive or because it is unnecessary, and that mankind can live and cooperate without the need of law enforcement.

The origins of anarchism are as follows:

- Philosophical anarchism, arising from ideas about human nature and the nature of society, is associated with Jean-Jacques Rousseau (1712–78) and William Godwin (1756–1836). Both saw mankind as capable of being made morally perfect if society were reformed and replaced by liberty.
- Communism, which flourished in the nineteenth century, was the belief that mankind should return to natural, self-governing and self-reliant communities. This is most associated with Peter Kropotkin (1842–1921).
- Collectivism, which is also associated with socialism, is a belief that humankind is naturally social and prefers to achieve goals collectively rather than individually. Mikhail Bakunin (1814–76) is a typical example of an anarchist holding this view.
- Individualism is a view that mankind is not fundamentally social but prefers to be able to exercise his or her individuality freely. All social and political constraints are seen as unnatural and oppressive. Typical examples of anarchists in this tradition are Henry Thoreau (1817–62) and Max Stirner (1806–56). Murray Rothbard (1926–95) is a more recent example.

> **Exam tip**
>
> As with any discussion of an ideology, you should be able to quote the ideas of several specific anarchist thinkers, including all the key thinkers, to illustrate the points you are making.

Core ideas of anarchism

Human nature

REVISED

On the whole, anarchists have come to five different conclusions about human nature:

1 People are basically self-interested or egoistical and will cooperate with other people only if they believe it to be in their own interests.
2 People are naturally sociable and altruistic, and prefer to cooperate rather than compete with each other.
3 People are born without any basic nature. We are, in fact, a *tabula rasa*, a blank surface on which society, with all its faults, writes our character. Put another, more contemporary, way, human nature is environmentally determined.
4 People are born 'good' in that they are sociable and rational and take into account the interests of others when making decisions, preferring **altruism** to selfishness. This also implies that we are naturally social, that we prefer to live and work cooperatively in natural groups rather than compete with each other as individuals.
5 Humankind has the capacity for goodness and morality but needs to be educated and to live in a morally perfect society for this to be realised.

> **Altruism** The belief that humankind is not born to be self-seeking but can display fellow-feeling, sympathy for others and an instinct to help and cooperate with others. Most, though not all, anarchists espouse the idea of altruism.

Table 5.1 summarises these views of human nature and gives an example of an anarchist thinker associated with the view described.

Table 5.1 Anarchism and human nature

Anarchist view of human nature	Example(s)
Humankind is fundamentally egotistical and self-interested, feeling a sense of personal entitlement for all the fruits of the earth.	Max Stirner
Humankind is naturally cooperative and not competitive.	Peter Kropotkin
Humankind has no innate character — how we behave is a product of the society in which we have grown up.	Mikhail Bakunin
People are born good and if society is transformed, the innate goodness of humankind will prevail.	William Godwin
People are capable of being perfected, largely through moral education.	Jean-Jacques Rousseau

Key thinker

Max Stirner (1806–56)

Stirner was a key figure in the development of individualist anarchism. He is also known for the anarchist theory of egoism and was a key figure in the movement known as nihilism.

The main ideas of Max Stirner were as follows:
- He believed that the driving force behind human nature is the self-interested ego.
- In the book *The Ego and His Own* (1845) he expressed his theory of egoism.
- He called religions and ideologies **'spooks and ghosts'**, meaning they were illusions and distortions of truth.
- The exercise of the unrestricted ego would challenge the authority of the state.
- His idea for a **'union of egoism'** was to spread such individualism so that state and religion would be destroyed and replaced.
- He asserted that individuals are entitled to everything that exists in the world.
- Individuals would have a common interest in such egoism and this would create some kind of order.
- He believed in revolutionary change.
- He advocated complete, unrestricted individual liberty.
- He proposed that the state be brought down through violent **insurrection**. This was to be an all-out attack on all the organs of the state.

Exam tip

Be careful to distinguish clearly between different anarchist perceptions of human nature. Some anarchists view human nature as fundamentally good and altruistic, some see humankind as fundamentally self-interested and egoistic, while some see humankind as corrupted by society but capable of being made perfect through education and moral enlightenment.

Insurrection A term used by anarchists and other revolutionaries to describe any direct action, usually violent, designed to bring down the state.

Revision activity

Look at these anarchist thinkers. In each case describe their view of human nature.
1 Max Stirner.
2 Peter Kropotkin.
3 Henry Thoreau.

Exam practice answers and quick quizzes at
www.hoddereducation.co.uk/myrevisionnotesdownloads

The state

All anarchists, of course, oppose the state and propose its abolition. However, there are a number of different reasons why anarchists have opposed the state:

- It is evil and oppressive. It denies the individual their freedom and individualism.
- It is unnecessary. Humankind is capable of maintaining a harmonious social order without a state, **government** or oppressive laws.
- The modern **state** is associated with capitalism, which is divisive and exploitive. Capitalism is, for most though not all anarchists, a system which creates conflict and corrupts human nature.
- The state is associated with organised religion. Anti-clericalism among anarchists is based on the idea that religion robs people of their individualism and, ultimately, their liberty.

The anarchist objection to the democratic state is more complex and is based on these principles:

- **Direct democracy** is unacceptable as it represents the tyranny of a majority.
- People cannot be justified in giving away their personal sovereignty to the **authority** and **power** of the state.
- Government by consent is not acceptable as the people are unable to withdraw their consent. Furthermore, one generation cannot consent on behalf of future generations.
- Representative democracy is opposed on the grounds that it is not acceptable that some individuals should govern on behalf of others. It is a denial of individual sovereignty.

> **Government** Represents the institutions that exercise power over us. For anarchists, governments, even democratic ones, cannot be justified and have no authority to exercise power over us.
>
> **State** For anarchists, the concentration of coercive power in political institutions. States are to be opposed on the grounds that they are either unnecessary or coercive and deny our individual liberty.

> **Direct democracy** A system of government where the people make all important decisions themselves and do not rely upon representatives to do so.
>
> **Authority** The right to exercise power. In democratic theory, people can grant authority to government to exercise power over them. Anarchists reject this. We cannot grant the authority to exercise power over us as this is a denial of our individual sovereignty.
>
> **Power** The ability to force people to do something or prevent them from doing something. For anarchists, power can never be justified and is always coercive. The state exercises unjustifiable power.

> **Revision activity**
>
> Consider these anarchists. In each case describe the nature of their opposition to the state:
> 1 William Godwin.
> 2 Mikhail Bakunin.
> 3 Emma Goldman.

Society

Anarchists differ widely on how they conceive society without a state. Table 5.2 summarises how different anarchist traditions and thinkers view the ideal society.

Table 5.2 Anarchism and society

Form of society	Anarchist tradition	Associated anarchist thinkers
A society of free, voluntary communities which are self-governing and based on common ownership of property and economic equality. This will preserve both **autonomy** and society.	Anarcho-communism	Peter Kropotkin
A society divided into communities based on occupations, cooperating and trading with each other on the basis of mutual benefit.	Federalism	Mikhail Bakunin
A society based on largely individual craft workers who work on their own account and exchange goods with each other on the basis of the value of labour input rather than market value.	Mutual aid	Pierre-Joseph Proudhon
The state to be replaced by a series of trade union-based socialist organisations constructed on the basis of common ownership and shared rewards.	Anarcho-syndicalism	Georges Sorel
No social organisations at all, with individuals becoming largely self-sufficient and cooperating only where strictly necessary.	Individualism	Henry Thoreau
A society where all individuals operate in an independent manner and seek to pursue their own interests. The balance of self-interests will form a kind of harmony.	Union of egoists	Max Stirner
An intensely competitive capitalist society where each individual or company pursues its own objectives in a free-market situation.	Anarcho-capitalism	Murray Rothbard

> **Autonomy** Represents the absence of any artificial external constraints, though not necessarily internal restraints. All anarchists believe that humankind should be able to exercise autonomy.

Key thinker

Peter Kropotkin (1842–1921)

Kropotkin was arguably the key figure in anarcho-communism.

The main ideas of Peter Kropotkin were as follows:

- He viewed mankind as a fundamentally social animal.
- He drew inspiration from the animal kingdom which he saw as basically social, as opposed to Darwinian theories of life as a constant struggle for survival and dominance.
- Capitalism created a Darwinian world which Kropotkin believed was not natural.
- His theory of **mutual aid** reflected a belief that humankind is naturally cooperative.
- He advocated the creation of natural, small-scale, self-sufficient communities.
- In such communities there would be no private property and absolute economic equality.
- Communities would trade with each other on mutually beneficial terms. This was expressed in his great work, *Fields, Factories and Workshops* (1912).

> **Mutual aid** A term used by many anarchists to mean that communities should cooperate with each other, largely in terms of trade, on mutually beneficial terms rather than through a free-market mechanism.

Exam practice answers and quick quizzes at
www.hoddereducation.co.uk/myrevisionnotesdownloads

The economy

Anarchism's attitude to economic life is critical to an understanding of the ideology. There are many different attitudes to the economy within anarchism, but all anarchists hold in common the following features:

● It is desirable to establish economic freedom.
● Economic relations between people and organisations should be the result of free negotiation.
● As the state would be abolished, there would be no external regulation of trade or finance. Taxation would cease to exist and there would be no 'public goods' such as police, transport, defence, etc.

However, there are also important distinctions between different strands of anarchism. These include the following:

● While most anarchists propose the abolition of private property, some, such as Stirner, Proudhon and Rothbard, accept that personal property is a necessity.
● Some anarchists, notably communists and early American individualists like Thoreau, propose a return to 'simpler' forms of economic life. Others, like Bakunin, accept the inevitability of industrialisation.
● Anarchists differ in their proposals for how goods are to be exchanged. Some, like Proudhon, developed scientific ways of establishing the 'true' value of goods, largely based on the amount of labour used; others, such as anarcho-capitalists, see value based on free-market forces, while a third group, including collectivists and communists, see the establishment of value being based on free negotiations between buyers and sellers on the basis of 'mutual' benefit.

Table 5.3 summarises the economic attitudes of different strands of anarchism.

Table 5.3 Anarchism and the economy

Strands of anarchism	Typical economic attitudes
Individualist anarchism	As far as possible people should be self-sufficient. Subsistence-type economies are supported in this tradition. Trade should be undertaken only where necessary. The terms of such trade should be freely negotiated.
Egoism	The ego is so strong that it is natural for all individuals to feel entitled to possess all the earth's products. The constant state of competition will create a kind of dynamic tension, resulting in economic harmony.
Anarcho-communism	Membership of economic communities should be voluntary. They should be self-sufficient as far as possible, but trade with each other on mutually beneficial terms.
Federalism	Large economic federations should be formed, possibly based upon occupational groups. The value of labour and its products should be based on the value of labour inputs and not market values. In other words, goods should be priced on the basis of how much labour has gone into producing them.
Syndicalism	This is similar to federalism, but the social groupings are to be based on trade union organisations and therefore on occupations and crafts.
Anarcho-capitalism	A modern version of egoism. All economic activity should be free of state interference. All markets, for labour, for products and for finance, should be completely free. Social harmony is guaranteed by the natural harmony within free-market systems.

Different types of anarchism

Anarchism and utopianism

Anarchism has both positive and negative connections with the term 'utopianism'.

Positive aspects

- Anarchists are proposing an ideal society. This is common to most ideologies.
- Anarchists, on the whole, hold an optimistic view of human nature. If their optimistic view is accurate, an ideal society with peace, equality and harmony is possible.
- It is the anarchist view that modern societies are all corrupted by such negative factors as the exercise of power, denial of freedom, inequality and economic exploitation. The removal of such corruptions, say anarchists, makes a utopia a realistic objective.

Negative aspects

- Critics, notably fundamentalist socialists, claim that there is no scientific basis for an anarchist utopia, that it is based on unrealisable dreams.
- Various anarchists have proposed very different versions of utopia, which calls into question whether any of them is based on rational ideas.
- Similarly, critics point to the variations in anarchist views on human nature, again calling into question the rationality of their ideas.
- Some critics accept the desirability of many anarchist goals but are sceptical whether they can be achieved. Above all, they believe that a society without a state will fall into disharmony at best, chaos and violence at worst. They point to the existence of many modern 'failed states' to illustrate this criticism.

> **Typical mistake**
>
> Do not assume that when anarchism is described as 'utopian', this is a criticism. Utopianism can be a positive as well as a negative idea.

Collectivist forms of anarchism

Collectivist anarchists hold the following beliefs in common:
- That humankind is fundamentally social in nature.
- That we prefer to achieve goals collectively rather than individually.
- That there should be common ownership of wealth and goods.
- That society should be based on equality.

Despite these common beliefs, there are various strands of collectivist anarchism. These include the following.

Communism

- Peter Kropotkin and Errico Malatesta were leading advocates.
- Based on the idea than mankind is naturally social.
- Advocated the replacement of the centralised state by small-scale natural communities (communes) where membership was voluntary and property was held communally.
- Experimental versions appeared in the Jura mountains of Switzerland among watchmakers (the Jura Federation) in the later nineteenth century.
- Similar to the Marxist idea of the final stage of history with a stateless, classless society.
- Communes would trade with each other on a mutually beneficial basis.

> **Typical mistake**
>
> The term 'communism' is usually associated with Marxism. This association is correct, but many anarchists also describe themselves as communist. This is because both are proposing the formation of voluntary, self-governing communities.

Exam practice answers and quick quizzes at
www.hoddereducation.co.uk/myrevisionnotesdownloads

Mutualism

- Similar to anarcho-communism.
- Its main advocates included Pierre-Joseph Proudhon, Emma Goldman and Elisée Reclus.
- Goods should be exchanged on the basis of the value of labour put into making them, not their market value.
- Mutualists advocated small collective organisations operating normally on the basis of similar crafts.
- Based on the idea of 'brotherhood' which arises from working together.
- Some artistic communities today still practise mutualism and are known as 'collectives'.

Syndicalism

- Similar to mutualism.
- Believes that the state can be replaced by trade union-based federations.
- Associated with violent nineteenth-century revolutionary Georges Sorel, and Rudolf Rocker in the early twentieth century.
- A very revolutionary tradition which advocates **direct action** to bring down the state.
- Common occupations breed natural brotherhood.

Collectivist anarchism has often been described as 'socialism without a state' or merely a decentralised form of socialism. Table 5.4 summarises the relationship between anarchism and socialism.

Direct action A reference to people taking action to undermine and ultimately destroy the state. Such action is described as direct when it includes such methods as violence, civil disobedience and propaganda.

Typical mistake

It is tempting to believe that individualist anarchists are proposing the destruction of society as well as the state. This is not necessarily so. Some such anarchists believe that intense individualism can exist within the context of social harmony.

Table 5.4 Anarchism and socialism

Arguments that anarchism is socialism without a state	Counter-arguments
Both anarchism and socialism are critiques of the capitalist state.	Socialism is a doctrine of social **solidarity** while anarchists mainly wish to restore individual liberty.
The two ideologies share an optimistic view of human nature — that humankind is capable of cooperation without coercion.	While communists and collectivist anarchists propose collective ownership, anarcho-individualists accept the existence of private property.
Most anarchists propose economic equality and common ownership of property.	While socialism is a class-based ideology, anarchists are concerned less with class, more with the restoration of individual sovereignty.
Communism is the end goal of both fundamentalist socialists and many anarchists.	Anarchist communism is based on the idea of small, pastoral communities while socialist communism is proposed within industrial society.

Solidarity A term shared by socialists, collectivist anarchists and communists. It refers to a natural tendency or desire for humans to form themselves into close-knit groups for the purposes of revolution and, after revolution, of creating new communities.

Revision activity

Consider these anarchist thinkers. Explain their main views on what social order should replace the state:
1 Mikhail Bakunin.
2 Pierre-Joseph Proudhon.

Key thinker

Pierre-Joseph Proudhon (1809–65)

Famous for his book *What Is Property?* (1840) and his slogan **'property is theft'**, Proudhon is believed to have first developed the term 'anarchism'. As such he is the founder of modern anarchism.

The main ideas of Pierre-Joseph Proudhon were as follows:

- He distinguished between 'property,' which is used to exploit others, and 'possessions', which are not and can therefore be justified.

- He was not a revolutionary but envisaged a peaceful, possibly parliamentary transition to anarchism.
- His theories are sometimes considered to be a form of decentralised socialism without a state.
- He envisaged workers engaging in free contracts with each other to exchange goods.
- His ideas, known as mutualism, are based on a highly optimistic view of human nature, proposing that free relationships will result in an absence of exploitation.
- He influenced the cooperative movement and proposed subsistence forms of production in poorer societies.

Key thinker

Mikhail Bakunin (1814–76)

Bakunin was known as a collectivist anarchist, famous for his theories of federalism. He was close to the Marxists until the 1870s when Marxism and anarchism split for ever.

The main ideas of Mikhail Bakunin were as follows:

- He was violently anti-capitalist and saw the state as the agent of the capitalist class.
- Unlike the Marxists he advocated the abolition of the state and the immediate transition to a stateless society (inspired by the short-lived experience of the Paris Commune in 1871).

- He asserted that power not only oppresses people, but also corrupts those who exercise it.
- He believed in the concept of natural law to which all people are subject. In a stateless society, natural law would take over.
- He advocated a system of federalism in which workers would divide themselves into communities where there would be no private property and total economic equality.
- The federations would trade with each other on mutually negotiated terms, based on the labour value of goods instead of their market value.

Key thinker

Emma Goldman (1869–1940)

Goldman was an anarchist, a revolutionary and a feminist. She was a romantic rather than an ideological thinker and so has been accused of intense utopianism.

The main ideas of Emma Goldman were as follows:

- She believed in violent revolution and assassinations to bring down the state.
- As a revolutionary, she believed that actions speak louder than words so the best form of propaganda is violence.

- She was a feminist as well as an anarchist and believed that women will be emancipated only when the state is abolished.
- She developed the concept of mutual love to replace the competitive world of capitalism. As such she was a romantic thinker.
- Like Bakunin she saw the state as the managing committee of capitalism (as well as patriarchy).
- She advocated an individualist social order where society would be held together not by the state, laws or an economic system but by mutual love and respect.

Now test yourself

1 Identify the key term associated with anarchism which is described in each of these cases:
   (a) William Godwin's idea that, without compulsion, moral human beings will be able to use their own reason to arrive at moral solutions to social questions.
   (b) The name of Kropotkin's theory that communities can cooperate to their mutual benefit.
   (c) The name often given to Bakunin's brand of anarchism.
   (d) The name given to Stirner's theory of anarchism.
2 Explain the distinction between Bakunin's and Marx's view of the state.

Answers on p. 110

Individualist forms of anarchism

Individualist anarchists hold the following beliefs in common:
- A person is not naturally social but is naturally an individual.
- The state and other forms of social organisation are a denial of individual sovereignty.
- Freedom is not compatible with society.

Despite these common beliefs, there are various strands of individualist anarchism.

The American individualist tradition

- Associated with such nineteenth-century practitioners as Henry Thoreau, Lysander Spooner and Josiah Warren, all Americans.
- Such anarchists recommend that individuals withdraw from society, living alone or in kinship groups.
- As far as possible people should become self-sufficient to avoid excessive social interaction.
- Where interaction is necessary it should be peaceful and mutually beneficial.

Egoism

- Associated with Max Stirner.
- There is a belief that people are naturally egotistical.
- Stirner and his followers believed that individuals are entitled to lay claim to the fruits of the earth.
- There will be social harmony when egoism becomes widespread and a union of egoists will be formed where dynamic harmony will ensue.
- Possibly the most revolutionary form of anarchism.

Anarcho-capitalism

- A largely modern movement from the later twentieth century onwards.
- Associated with Robert Nozick and Murray Rothbard.
- It promotes the idea of completely free-market capitalism.
- There should be no state at all or a very limited state that does not interfere in economic activity. .
- Individuals should be free to succeed or fail in such a system.
- The competition generated in such a system will create wealth effectively and society will become economically dynamic.

Exam tip

Anarcho-capitalism is sometimes seen as a form of ultra-conservatism. It is, but it is also a modern version of individualist anarchism. It belongs in both traditions.

Individualist anarchism has often been described as an 'extreme form of liberalism'. Table 5.5 summarises the relationship between anarchism and liberalism.

Table 5.5 Anarchism and liberalism

Arguments that anarchism is merely extreme liberalism	Arguments that anarchism is fundamentally different to liberalism
Both anarchists and liberals place individual liberty at the centre of their belief system.	Anarchists insist on the abolition of the state while liberals see the state as the guarantor of liberty.
Both anarchists and liberals see the state as the potential enemy of individual liberty.	Liberals broadly support free-market capitalism while most (not all) anarchists oppose capitalism.
Both have adopted an optimistic view of human nature, believing that humankind can potentially use freedom for good ends.	Liberals see property ownership as natural, while most (not all) anarchists propose common ownership of property.
Anarcho-capitalism can be seen as an extreme form of liberalism.	Most liberals see inequality as natural while most anarchists wish to promote absolute equality. However, anarcho-capitalists share a belief in natural inequality with liberals.
Anarchists and liberals both promote the idea of social justice.	Individualist anarchists believe that social justice is the normal outcome of a free society.

Exam tip

One of the most difficult concepts in anarchism is that of freedom. You need to be able to distinguish between the typical anarchist perspective on freedom and that of typical liberals. You also need to be able to explain how collectivist anarchists can reconcile the need for individual freedom with the instinct for social forms of organisation.

Tensions within anarchism

REVISED

The following are the main tensions that exist among different strands of anarchist thought. In each case they are linked to one of the four key themes of human nature, society, the economy and the state.

Human nature

- Anarchists differ over whether people are born with a sense of morality, fellow-feeling and altruism, whether they are born egotistical and self-interested, or whether they are born without any traits at all but their character is determined by the kind of society in which they live.
- Some argue that humankind prefers to achieve goals collectively while others claim we prefer to pursue our goals individually.
- Some anarchists believe that social groups are natural, while others take a Darwinian view of human life where there is intense competition.

The state

- Some anarchists, such as William Godwin, simply believe that the state is unnecessary once a totally moral society has been created, while others are less optimistic and believe the existing state must be destroyed in one blow.

- Anarcho-capitalists accept the need for a minimal state, while most anarchists strongly believe that the whole state must be completely abolished.
- Anarchists such as Bakunin see the state largely as the managing committee of capitalism, so that the abolition of capitalism would also result in the end of the state. Others, however, see the state largely as a political body exercising power in any context.

Society

- Individualist anarchists deny that society is natural and would either abolish social organisations or recommend that individuals withdraw from society.
- Some collectivist anarchists propose small-scale social communities based on voluntary, natural membership, while others prefer communities based on common occupations.
- For egoists, there can be no such thing as society in the conventional sense of the word, while all collectivist anarchists propose the creation of some kind of society.

The economy

- Nearly all anarchists propose the abolition of private property, though some, such as Proudhon, would allow personal possessions and small-scale, privately owned industry and the anarcho-capitalists support private property.
- While most anarchists propose the abolition of market-based systems of establishing the value of goods and labour, anarcho-capitalists see the market system as fundamental to human life.
- There are both anarcho-communists and individualist anarchists who propose a return to simple, subsistence-based economic structures, but many anarchists also accept industrialisation and large-scale production, within an anarchist context.

> **Typical mistake**
>
> Do not assume that all anarchists oppose the state only because it is evil and coercive. In fact, some anarchists believe the state is simply unnecessary.

> **Revision activity**
>
> Explain why anarchists have considered the state:
> - unnecessary
> - unacceptably coercive.

> **Exam tip**
>
> When discussing the extent to which anarchism is a single movement or a series of different movements, it is important that you have a thorough grasp of what unites all anarchists and not just what divides them.

> ## Now test yourself
>
> TESTED
>
> 3 What is the view of human nature associated with these key thinkers?
>   (a) Peter Kropotkin.
>   (b) Henry Thoreau.
>   (c) Emma Goldman.
>   (d) Mikhail Bakunin.
>
> Answers on p. 110

Anarchism today

REVISED

It is tempting to view anarchism purely as an historical phenomenon. However, anarchism still exists as an ideological tradition in a number of ways:

- Anarcho-capitalism, exemplified by the ideas of Robert Nozick in the USA, is flourishing and has become a respectable, though minority, political view.
- Influenced by E.F. Schumacher, many environmentalists see themselves as part of the anarchist tradition. They believe that it will be necessary to move to a more natural, subsistence kind of society, similar to that

proposed by anarcho-communists, in order to save the environment from disaster.

● The anti-capitalist movement that grew in the early part of the twenty-first century has been inspired by the ideas of anarchism.

● Some radical feminists see themselves as anarchists. They view the state as fundamentally patriarchal, so its abolition is necessary to defeat patriarchy and to establish female consciousness in society.

Now test yourself

TESTED

4 Identify:
   (a) three ideas that unite all anarchists
   (b) three ideas that divide anarchists.
5 Identify three concepts associated with anarcho-capitalism.

Answers on p. 110

Typical mistake

Though anarchism has never succeeded in the sense that a movement has replaced an actual state, it remains influential. Do not assume it is merely hypothetical — it still influences a number of social movements, including environmentalism, anti-capitalism and feminism.

Exam practice

You must use appropriate thinkers you have studied to support your answer and consider both sides in a balanced way.

1 To what extent is anarchism a single movement? [24]
2 To what extent can anarchism be described as nothing more than socialism without a state? [24]
3 To what extent can anarchism be seen as nothing more than an extreme form of liberalism? [24]

Answers and quick quiz 5 online

ONLINE

Summary

You should now have an understanding of:
● the distinction between individualist and collectivist anarchism
● various anarchist views of human nature
● the different reasons why anarchists in general oppose the state
● the relationship between anarchism and utopianism

● whether anarchism can be described as a single movement or a series of different traditions
● the differences between anarchism and extreme liberalism
● the differences between anarchism and socialism
● the relationship between anarchism and capitalism.

6 Nationalism

The origins of nationalism

The term 'nationalism' refers to political ideas and movements which have the interests and advancement of the nation as their central theme, inspiration and aspiration.

- Liberal revolutionaries in the eighteenth century sought a basis for new democratic political communities to replace territories controlled by hereditary monarchs. They identified the nation as the most appropriate form of political community.
- Also in the eighteenth century, a number of conservative thinkers saw the world as naturally divided into nations based on common culture and language.
- In the age of European empires, nationalism took root among peoples seeking freedom from imperial control. This applied to subject peoples in the Austro-Hungarian Empire, such as Hungary and parts of Italy, as well as parts of the Ottoman Empire.
- Some peoples who had become divided into different states, such as the Germans, Italians and Slavs, instituted unity movements based on common national identity.
- Nineteenth-century moderate conservative movements in such countries as Britain and France stressed nationalism as a means of creating patriotism and an organic society.

Key thinker

Jean-Jacques Rousseau (1712–78)

Rousseau is not normally described as a nationalist but his ideas were taken up by French revolutionary nationalists and republicans at the end of the eighteenth century.

The main ideas of Jean-Jacques Rousseau which are relevant to nationalism were as follows:

- In terms of the creation of states, he believed that patriotism and civic pride were vital qualities needed to reinforce the nation.
- Being concerned with how government should be formed, he asserted that national identity must be the basis of the political community.

- Only people with such a national identity would enjoy sufficient unity to be able to create a single consciousness.
- Rousseau's idea of the nation was a romantic one in the sense that he recognised the existence of some kind of national 'spirit' which could unite a people and form the basis of a democracy.
- As a liberal he believed in freedom, but mainly the collective freedom of a people.
- He was a republican who would only accept government by the collective consent of the people.
- His philosophy, sometimes described as **rationalism**, provides a rational justification for the political existence of the nation.

Typical mistake

Though Rousseau is associated with early nationalism, he is predominantly a democratic, liberal thinker. His nationalism merely underpinned his ideas of 'government by consent'. He should be treated not as a pioneer of nationalism but as a philosophical antecedent of liberal nationalism.

Rationalism A kind of philosophy or ideology based on rational ideas rather than romantic sentiments.

Core ideas of nationalism

Human nature

The relationship between nationalism and human nature is based on the idea that there are social, cultural and ethnic forces that bind people together. The key examples of such forces include the following:

- **Language:** associated with German thinkers such as Johann Herder and Johann Fichte, language is seen as the key feature of common culture. Peoples who are scattered may come together on the basis of common language. A key example is German nineteenth-century nationalism.
- **Religion:** this can cross existing state and national boundaries. A people see themselves as defined by their common religion. Jewish Zionism is a key example, as is radical modern Islamic nationalism.
- **Culture and history:** people may feel they have a common history and common cultural traits. Culture transcends such features as **ethnicity** and religion. A shared historical experience is important. Scottish and Italian nationalism are key examples.
- **Ethnicity:** national identity is based on ethnicity and race. It is **exclusive** in that nationality is reserved to members of a race. A key example is Chinese nationalism.
- **Geography:** nationalism is associated with traditional territory. It is inclusive in that it can encompass members of different religions and ethnic groupings. Russian nationalism is a key example.

Cultural nationalism is a key aspect of the relationship between human nature and nationalism. This includes a number of features and examples:

- Liberal cultural nationalism, such as Welsh or Catalan nationalism, is concerned with the protection of a culture through democratic institutions and the ideal of liberty.
- Conservative nationalism, which has flourished in the UK, is a moderate emotion which seeks to preserve an organic society united by a shared sense of history and culture. It may also see its culture as superior to nationalist other cultures. Such nationalists harness patriotism to their cause.
- Ultra conservative cultural nationalism sees its characteristics as superior to others. It may take an expansionist form, as was the case with radical German nationalism under the Nazi Party in the 1930s and 1940s. It may also be defensive when threatened by other cultures, as has been the case with Chinese nationalism. The term **Volksgeist** expresses the idea among such conservative nationalists that there is such a thing as national spirit which transcends individual consciousness.

Human nature is also linked with nationalism through racism and racialism. Racism takes these forms:

- It believes that a racial group is the basis of nationhood and the nation should be exclusive to those who are members of that race.
- It usually sees the race in question as superior to other races.
- In multiracial societies, racism takes the form of discrimination and sometimes oppression of other races.
- Racism flourished in Nazi Germany and has been seen in the form of white supremacy in the USA and the South African apartheid movement.

Ethnicity A term closely associated with racial identity. It stresses one's place of origin rather than one's specific race. It is also often used to refer to people who are living among a people of a different origin.

Exclusive nationalism A belief that citizenship of a nation or the assumption of national identity requires an individual to enjoy common culture, race or language with the existing members of the nation.

Volksgeist A German expression, associated with conservatism, which refers to the spirit of the nation, a force which unites people and gives them a strong sense of national identity.

Typical mistake

Do not assume that cultural nationalism is always expansionist because Nazism was described as 'cultural' in nature. Cultural nationalists can be moderate and concerned with autonomy rather than conquest. Welsh nationalism is an example of such moderate nationalism.

Key thinker

Johann Gottfried von Herder (1744–1803)

Herder was known as a 'romantic' thinker, part of a wider philosophical movement in Europe that reacted against the rational ideas of the Enlightenment.

The main ideas of Johann Gottfried von Herder which are relevant to nationalism were as follows:
- He believed that a common language was a key feature of nationalist sentiment.
- Further, he argued that a nation could be defined by its common language.
- A national language also expresses the common culture of a people and so, Herder claimed, a nation can be defined by its culture.

- He described the common culture and spirit of a people as their *Volksgeist*.
- He was especially concerned that the German people be defined by their language and that this could form the basis of a united German people in one state (at a time when Germany was divided into many individual states).
- Nationalism should be based not on rational ideas, as Rousseau had argued, but on romantic, emotional idealism.
- Herder is very much seen as a 'conservative' nationalist and an inspiration behind the reunification of Germany which occurred in 1871 under Bismarck.

Racialism includes these features:
- It is neutral and does not necessarily see one race as superior to others.
- It does, however, see the division of the world into different races as natural and inevitable.
- Racialists see race and culture as strongly tied together.
- Japanese nationalism before the Second World War was a key example.

Nativism is a modern form of conservative cultural nationalism. It includes:
- a belief that the indigenous or original members of the state have a superior claim to wealth and property over groups who have migrated later into the state
- a strong belief in the protection of the state's economy from foreign competition
- opposition to large-scale immigration which, nativists believe, will 'destabilise' society.

It has been seen in such movements as US President Donald Trump's brand of populist conservatism in the USA, the UK Independence Party and Marine Le Pen's French Front National Party.

The state

REVISED

Nationalism and self-determination
- The idea of the self-determination of peoples arose in the eighteenth century as part of the Enlightenment.
- It was associated with Jean-Jacques Rousseau.
- Self-determination could be achieved only if hereditary monarchy was overthrown.
- The political community was defined by the existence of the nation.
- It also depended upon the development of government by consent and some form of democracy.
- The synthesis of self-determination, anti-monarchy, democracy and government by consent became widely known as republicanism.

> **Typical mistake**
>
> Although republicanism involves opposition to hereditary monarchy, that is not its only emotion. Republicans also insist that liberal democracy must be associated with nationalist aspirations.

The state and the nation

The terms 'state' and 'nation' are linked but must always be distinguished:

- The state is a political reality. It is the existence of a monopoly of coercive power in one single authority.
- It exists as long as a people consent to be governed by its institutions.
- A nation is a people who consider themselves to have common circumstances of birth.
- Nations may exist independently of states, for example Scotland.
- Some states exist without coinciding with national identity.
- States may be multinational (the UK) or can be artificial creations with no particular relationship to a nation (Australia).

The nation-state

- The nation-state became the basis for nearly all modern states.
- This dates back to the early twentieth century.
- The Versailles conference in 1919 declared the right of all nation-states to independent existence.
- Nation-states depend on **civic nationalism** for their survival.

Internationalism

This is the synthesis of an independent people, democratic institutions, absence of monarchy and government by consent.

- Internationalism is either liberal or socialist in nature.
- It is a denial of the primacy of nation-states.
- As a doctrine it seeks to break down divisions between people based on separate states and separate nations.

> **Typical mistake**
>
> Do not confuse nationalism with patriotism. Nationalism concerns a love of one's nation whereas patriotism is a love of the state in which an individual resides. It is possible, for example, to be a British patriot without being a British nationalist. It is also possible to be a Scottish nationalist without being a British patriot.

> **Exam tip**
>
> It is vital to understand that nation and state are different concepts. A nation is a people who have an identity based on shared birth or experience whereas a state is a political reality, a territory governed by a single authority. Nations can exist without being states, while states may not be nations or may be multinational.

> **Civic nationalism** An idea associated with Rousseau, this is connected with patriotism and proposes that nationalism should be based on a sense of civic pride. It also implies that a free people are collectively as well as individually free.

Society

REVISED

There are a number of movements that propose a society which can exist outside national identity. Three examples are as follows:

- Civic nationalism concerns the creation of national pride without the existence of a single nation with a common history. It can be described as **inclusive nationalism**. The typical examples are the USA and Australia.
- **Liberal internationalism** seeks to break down national boundaries on the basis that the nation-state is a denial of liberty.

> **Inclusive nationalism** A belief that any individual can assume a national identity without having any special attachment to that nation, such as race or culture or even language.
>
> **Liberal internationalism** A view that national boundaries should be de-emphasised and that international cooperation is crucial to social and economic progress.

- **Socialist internationalism** seeks to break down national boundaries on the basis that class identity should transcend national divisions.

There is a synoptic link between nationalism and multiculturalism. The relationship between nationalism and a multicultural society includes the following features:
- Multicultural theory suggests that a synthesis of different national identities in one society can be achieved without social conflict.
- Multiculturalism proposes that peoples with different cultural identities can nevertheless adopt a single value system.
- In a multicultural society, civic pride and patriotism are required to replace the unifying force of traditional nationalism.

> **Socialist internationalism**
> Socialists often oppose nationalism on the grounds that it is a dangerous rival to socialist consciousness. In order to combat this, many socialists advocate international cooperation and, in some circumstances, the destruction of national boundaries.

The economy

REVISED

The following examples show links between nationalism and economic ideas:
- Post-colonial nationalists seek to resist the penetration of their economies by multinational corporations.
- This leads many such nationalists to adopt state socialism to combat such penetrations.
- Cuba and Zambia are good examples of the synthesis between nationalism and socialism.
- Some nationalists seek to reduce external interference by opposing free trade and adopting protectionist measures.
- The modern phenomenon of nativism adopts protectionist policies to oppose the subversion of the nation by globalisation. The doctrines of Donald Trump are typical.

> **Exam tip**
>
> When answering questions about nationalism in general it is vital to illustrate your analysis with real-world examples, both of nationalist thinkers and of nationalist movements.

Now test yourself

TESTED

1 Identify the key term associated with nationalism which is described in each of these cases:
   (a) An exaggerated sense of national superiority.
   (b) A strong sense of love of one's state.
   (c) Any theory that proposes that racial differences are important.
   (d) A German word meaning national spirit.
   (e) A word that means nationalism that seeks to unite a scattered people.
2 Explain the differences between a state and a nation.

Answers on p. 110

Different types of nationalism

Liberal nationalism

REVISED

The key features of liberal nationalism are as follows, with examples:
- Originally influenced by the Enlightenment.
- Early ideas associated with Rousseau.
- Links national identity with freedom and democracy.
- Closely tied to the idea of the nation-state as the key element of government by consent.
- Also associated with republicanism, i.e. democratic government without hereditary monarchy.

Key thinker

Giuseppe Mazzini (1805–72)

Mazzini is often considered to be the father of Italian nationalism. He was a romantic, revolutionary figure who was willing to fight for his nationalist beliefs. He is regarded as the founder of a united Italy in the 1860s.

The main ideas of Giuseppe Mazzini were as follows:
- His 'Young Italy' movement was republican, determined to overthrow the monarchy.

- He asserted that a nation could consider itself free only if it were a pure democracy.
- Like Rousseau he recognised the importance of the romantic idea of national spirit.

His views came into conflict with liberalism in that he saw the collective freedom of the nation as a more important enterprise than the establishment of individual liberty.

- Often associated with national liberation movements (Austro-Hungarian Empire, modern Scottish and Catalan nationalism).
- Also associated with national unity movements — Mazzini and the Young Italy movement in the 1860s.

Liberal nationalism is normally seen as **progressive**, for these reasons:
- It is associated with the promotion of democracy.
- National self-determination is seen as essential for cultural, economic and social progress.
- Domination by external states is viewed as a barrier to national progress. This is very noticeable in modern Scottish nationalism.
- It rejects the past and looks to a future where there is democracy and liberty.

Progressive nationalism
Forms of nationalism that connect national autonomy and pride with improvements in the state of society and the economy.

> **Revision activity**
>
> Consider the contribution of the following to liberal nationalism:
> 1 Giuseppe Mazzini.
> 2 Jean-Jacques Rousseau.

Conservative nationalism

REVISED

The key forms of conservative nationalism are as follows.

Traditional nationalism

- Traditional nationalists fear that liberalism and an excess of individual liberty will weaken the unity of the nation.
- Such nationalists see the nation as organic rather than as a collection of individuals. The collective will of the people should take precedence over individualism.
- It is often associated with unifying movements, for example Germany under Bismarck and Garibaldi's nationalist Italian movement, both in the nineteenth century. Modern Russian nationalism is an example.
- Such conservatives tend to stress the exclusive nature of the nation and resist cultural and social diversity.

Regressive nationalists

- **Regressive nationalists** tend to be ultra-conservative.
- They believe the integrity of the nation is threatened both externally and internally.
- They tend to be xenophobic, fearing the influence of external states as well as groups inside society such as immigrants. In some cases they may be anti-semitic.
- They oppose excessively liberal ideas on the grounds that they threaten the organic nation.
- They tend to look back to an era when the nation was strong, unified and dominant.
- Examples include Maurras' French nationalism and Spanish inter-war fascism.

> **Exam tip**
>
> Make sure you understand that conservative nationalism is not a single movement but is a collective term for several different forms of nationalism.

Regressive nationalism
A description of forms of nationalism that look back to an age when a nation was successful and which hopes to recreate that situation.

> **Revision activity**
>
> Explain what is meant by regressive nationalism, with reference to the following:
> 1 Charles Maurras.
> 2 Adolf Hitler.

Exam practice answers and quick quizzes at
www.hoddereducation.co.uk/myrevisionnotesdownloads

Key thinker

Charles Maurras (1868–1952)

French nationalist Charles Maurras is known as the typical ultra-conservative form of nationalist. His brand of nationalism was imbued with racism and anti-semitism. His movement was known as *Action Française* and was intensely xenophobic.

The main ideas of Charles Maurras were as follows:
- He was anti-democratic and supported hereditary monarchy.
- He saw monarchy as a symbol of national power and pride.
- He laid a heavy stress on patriotism.

- His nationalism was reactionary as he yearned for a bygone age of French glory.
- He saw the French as a superior people and, as such, was a quasi-fascist. His views were often described as **chauvinism**.
- He was anti-semitic, very much as the German Nazis were.
- He believed that the collective identity of the people was a more important force than any drive towards individual liberty. Individualism should be suppressed in favour of collective national spirit.
- His brand of nationalism is sometimes described as **integral nationalism**, a denial of the individual will in favour of the collective will of the nation.

Nativists

- They share many of the traits of regressive nationalists.
- There is an emphasis on economic protectionism. In the modern context they are anti-free trade and globalisation.
- They have a strong sense of the superiority of original populations as against immigrant groups.
- They tend to be populists, opposing political establishments which are seen as weak and excessively liberal.
- They are also regressive in their view of national destiny.

Radical nationalists

- The basis of their nationalism is often racialist and racist.
- There is a strong sense of racial and national superiority.
- Nazism and Italian fascism are prominent examples.
- They tend to use mythology to create national identity rather than rationalism.
- Such movements claim to be progressive, seeing the nation moving towards a powerful, dominant future, but opponents see them as regressive, displaying an excessive obsession with past national glories.
- These movements are vehemently anti-liberal.

Imperialism

- This is largely historical.
- In the past, national progress was seen in terms of the creation of an overseas empire of colonial possessions.
- Britain, Germany, France, Spain, Japan and the Netherlands were prominent examples.
- Modern imperialism is largely confined to the idea of economic and political dominance of a region, as exemplified by modern Russia.

Chauvinist nationalism
An exaggerated emotion, suggesting that a particular nation is superior to other nations.

Integral nationalism
Associated with extreme right-wing nationalism, this denies the identity of the individual in favour of the interests of the whole nation.

Table 6.1 summarises the distinctions between progressive and regressive forms of nationalism.

Table 6.1 Progressive and regressive nationalism

Progressive	Regressive
Liberal nationalism has sought to establish the principles of democracy, tolerance and liberty.	Conservative nationalists often seek to re-create a 'golden era' from the past, thus preventing further development. Nations which constantly look back to their history for inspiration may find it difficult to react positively to modern developments. This was, for example, a major problem for Japanese nationalism after the Second World War as tradition clashed with modernity. China before communism is another example.
Liberal and socialist nationalists believe that it can be a force for progress, by uniting people around common values.	Conservative nationalism is often defensive and xenophobic and so sacrifices progress in favour of militarism and isolationism. One may view Donald Trump's form of populist nationalism in the USA from this perspective.
Liberal nationalists and republicans believe that the freedom of the nation is synonymous with the freedom of individuals; individual freedom is also seen as a prerequisite for cultural and economic progress.	Racial forms of nationalism, such as Nazism and Afrikaans' apartheid, can often exclude so-called 'inferior' racial groups from prominent roles in society and so lose their potentially positive contributions.
	The rise of nativism threatens economic progress by inhibiting trade and losing the efficiency which arises from competition.

Anti-colonial and post-colonial nationalism

REVISED ☐

These nationalist movements have flourished among nations that have freed themselves from colonial rule or which are resisting imperialism, including domination by global corporations. They tend to exhibit the following characteristics:

- They tend to have authoritarian governments on the basis that there is a need for a strong central authority to build national identity which has been suppressed by colonialism or imperialism.
- There is an imperative to build a national identity, based on 'liberation politics'.
- Most nationalist movements of this kind are socialist in character. The synthesis of nationalism and socialism is designed to create an economy which is independent of global capitalism.
- There are also examples of pan-nationalism where different people with common identities, such as race, tribe and culture, come together in a new national grouping that has not existed previously.
- Leadership cults are common. The character of the leader becomes a symbol of national unity.
- Pan-Africanism and pan-Arabism are prominent examples.

> **Exam tip**
>
> You should understand that although nationalism and fundamentalist socialism are normally seen as incompatible, many post-colonial nationalists are also socialists. This is because they aspire to resist international capitalism, which is a form of economic imperialism.

Key thinker

Marcus Garvey (1887–1940)

Garvey was Jamaican and, as such, was anti-colonialist.

The main ideas of Marcus Garvey were as follows:
- He developed the idea of black nationalism, a force which could unite all peoples of African origin.
- He was anti-colonial, seeing imperialism as the main obstacle to such black nationalism.
- He was a pan-nationalist, seeking to bring together all African nations.
- He was a major influence on the American black consciousness movement of the 1960s.
- He saw Ethiopia as the birthplace of all black peoples, giving them a common identity.

Table 6.2 summarises examples of post- and anti-colonial movements.

Table 6.2 Post- and anti-colonial movements

Anti-colonial leaders			
Leader	**Country**	**Colonial power**	**Political tradition**
Kwame Nkrumah (1909–72)	Ghana	Britain	Pan-Africanism
Frantz Fanon (1925–61)	Algeria	France	Marxism
Mahatma Gandhi (1869–1948)	India	Britain	Liberalism/social democracy
Gamal Abdel Nasser (1918–70)	Egypt	Britain/France	Pan-Arabism
Ho Chi Minh (1890–1969)	Vietnam	France	Maoist-style Marxism
Lee Kuan Yew (1923–2015)	Singapore	Britain	Conservatism
Patrice Lumumba (1925–61)	Congo	Belgium	Social democracy
Julius Nyerere (1922–99)	Tanzania	Britain	Community and kinship (Ujaama)
Robert Mugabe (1924–)	Zimbabwe	Britain	Moderate Marxism

Now test yourself

TESTED

3 Identify a key nationalist thinker associated with these ideas:
  (a) Black nationalism.
  (b) Civil pride.
  (c) Synthesising nationalism and socialism.
  (d) Synthesising radical nationalism and racism.
4 Explain the term 'radical nationalism'.

Answers on p. 110

Revision activity

Explain two forms of post-colonial nationalism, using the following references:
1 Fidel Castro.
2 Marcus Garvey.

Expansionist nationalism

REVISED

The main examples of expansionist nationalism are as follows:
- **Imperialism** is a form of nationalism that seeks to build an external empire. It can also be described as **colonialism**. This is largely historical.
- Pan-nationalism seeks to unite disparate peoples on the basis of race or culture to create a new national entity. Examples have been pan-Africanism, pan-Arabism and pan-Slavism.
- Militarism is where nationalism is synthesised with a desire for military conquest. In the case of the Nazis this was to increase the territory (so-called *Lebensraum*) used by Germanic peoples.

Imperialism/colonialism
A movement that involves a nation developing an overseas empire and which sees national progress in terms of building such an empire.

- Chauvinism is an exaggerated belief that one nation is superior to others. This kind of nationalism has flourished in France at various times, exemplified by Charles Maurras.
- Racism, the idea that a particular race is superior to others, has been a strong nationalist motivation. Nazism was the prime example, as was Japanese expansionism in the 1930s.

Black nationalism

REVISED

Black nationalism is a relatively modern movement. It has several characteristics:

- There is a belief in the common ancestry of black peoples in Africa, Ethiopia especially, which is viewed as the ancient cockpit of civilisation.
- It is associated with the idea of 'black consciousness'. This encompasses a collective identity based on a common experience of oppression and slavery.
- It had one practical application in the creation of the state of Liberia in North Africa, a home for freed slaves.
- Marcus Garvey was a key figure, influential in the West Indies and in the USA in the 1950s and 1960s.

> **Black nationalism** The idea that black people throughout the world are part of what is, effectively, a nation.

> **Exam tip**
>
> Examiners will expect you to understand that nationalists who seek to unite a people who have become scattered (so-called diaspora) are not always conservative. They can also be liberal, as is the case with many Zionists, or socialist, as is the case with many black nationalists.

> **Revision activity**
>
> Briefly explain the meaning of these terms:
> 1 Republicanism.
> 2 Racialism.
> 3 Nativism.

Now test yourself

TESTED

5 What kind of nationalism can be associated with these historical phenomena?
  (a) The reunification of Italy in the 1860s.
  (b) The Welsh desire for greater autonomy.
  (c) Liberation movements in Africa in the 1960s.
  (d) German fascism in the 1930s and 1940s.

Answers on p. 110

Tensions within nationalism

REVISED

The following are the key tensions within nationalism.

- **Romantic versus rational nationalism.** This broadly concerns the distinction between conservative forms and progressive, democratic forms.
- **Progressive versus regressive nationalism.** Progressive nationalist forms see their movements in terms of improving the state of the political community. This may involve a stronger democracy, firmer protection of human rights and economic development. Regressive nationalism reveres the past and hopes to see a return to a former 'golden age'. Improving the state therefore involves returning to political values from the past.

Exam practice answers and quick quizzes at
www.hoddereducation.co.uk/myrevisionnotesdownloads

- **Inclusive versus exclusive nationalism.** Inclusive nationalists place less stress on ethnicity, religion and common culture, accepting the idea of a multinational society united by common values. Exclusive nationalists insist that a nation should be the exclusive preserve of people with common ethnicity, religion and culture.
- **Expansionist nationalism versus nativism.** Expansionist nationalists see the destiny of the nation in terms of regional dominance or even imperialism. Nativists are inward looking, seeing national identity in terms of an exclusive society, undiluted by mixing with other national groupings.
- **Conservative versus liberal nationalism.** There are many variations of each kind of nationalism, but a generalised distinction is that conservatives see the nation as an organic whole, while liberals see the nation as free individuals with a shared identity.
- **Nationalism versus internationalism.** Nationalists see the world as being divided into national groups, each pursuing their own national interest. Internationalists de-emphasise national distinctions, preferring globalisation and the concept of 'common humanity'.
- **Racialism versus multiculturalism.** Racialists see the world in terms of racial divisions, with nations on the whole based on common ethnicity. In contrast, multiculturalists believe that different ethnic groups can co-exist within a single national entity. Common values are what unite people, for multiculturalists, rather than common ethnic and religious groupings.

Table 6.3 summarises distinctions between major forms of nationalism.

> **Typical mistake**
>
> Be careful not to confuse racism with racialism. Racism is an emotion that assumes one national identity or race is superior to another whereas racialism is a neutral term, describing any political or cultural theory about attributes enjoyed by members of different races.

> **Now test yourself**
>
> 6 In each case identify three distinctions between these forms of nationalism:
> (a) Progressive and regressive nationalism.
> (b) Liberal and conservative nationalism.
> (c) Racism and racialism.
>
> **Answers on p. 110–11**
>
> TESTED

Table 6.3 Key distinctions within nationalism

Liberal	Conservative	Post-colonial	Expansionist
It proposes the establishment of a liberal democracy in new nations.	It tends to stress the organic nature of the nation rather than individualism.	It is concerned less with creating a democratic state and more with nation building.	Expansionist nationalists do not respect the sovereignty of other nation-states.
The freedom of individuals is seen as synonymous with the freedom of the nation as a whole.	Patriotism is seen as a key social characteristic.	Post-colonial states are often socialist in order to combat economic imperialism from international capitalism.	There is usually a sense of racial or national superiority over other races and nations.
Liberal nationalists respect the sovereignty of other legitimate states.	Conservative states are either excessively defensive and seek to preserve national traditions or can be expansionist and seek to spread their national values to other peoples.	Post-colonial nationalists often synthesise nationalism with another political creed, such as socialism or religious fundamentalism. National community is stressed.	Such nation-states are often highly militaristic, stressing ideas of historic destiny and mythical heroism.
The liberal state is more important than the nation. Nationalism should serve the state.	The state exists to serve the interests of the organic nation.	Post-colonial nation-states are often subject to dictatorship in the interests of nation building and self-preservation.	The nation and its historic destiny transcend individualism and democracy.

Nationalism today

REVISED

There are various key issues in nationalism today:

- Nationalism stands in opposition to globalisation. Conservative, regressive forms of nationalism tend to oppose globalisation.
- The rise of nativism is a reaction to globalisation. Nativism breeds national protectionism, opposes the free migration of people and opposes internationalism.
- The division of the world into trading blocs, such as the European Union and the North American Free Trade Association (NAFTA), has been inhibited by the persistence of nationalist tendencies.
- In many cases, post-colonial nationalism has failed and given rise to 'failed states' where no common civic identity has been created.
- The synthesis of religion and pan-nationalism, notably within Islam, is now challenging western democratic and cultural values.

Exam practice

You must use appropriate thinkers you have studied to support your answer and consider both sides in a balanced way.

1 To what extent is nationalism a progressive movement? [24]
2 To what extent is right-wing nationalism associated with racism? [24]
3 To what extent is nationalism a cultural movement? [24]

Answers and quick quiz 6 online

ONLINE

Summary

You should now have an understanding of:
- the distinction between conservative and liberal forms of nationalism
- the distinction between the terms 'state' and 'nation'
- the role of racism in relation to nationalism
- the distinction between progressive and regressive nationalism
- the different forms of post- and anti-colonial nationalism
- the meaning of the term 'republicanism'.

7 Multiculturalism

The origins of multiculturalism

The idea of multiculturalism is a very modern one, becoming popular largely in the late twentieth and early twenty-first centuries. It is not really an ideology but rather a vision of how society is developing.

There are many, mostly liberals, who believe that multiculturalism is a positive development, and others, mostly conservative, who view it negatively.

- The increasing tendency of western societies to become multicultural has led to movements which have supported the change, seeing it as positive.
- Increasing globalisation and the free movement of peoples from diverse nationalities and cultures between states have created opportunities as well as tensions in modern society.
- The decline of colonial empires in Africa, Asia and the West Indies, in particular, led to mass movements of peoples from different racial and religious origins into developed western democracies.
- As multiculturalism became more common, a number of different conceptions of what multiculturalism can achieve began to emerge.
- The growth of tensions between various communities within states led to debates about how such states should respond to diversity.

Exam tip

Before you revise multiculturalism, make sure you have revised liberalism thoroughly. The key to understanding multiculturalism, as well as criticisms of it, lies in liberal thought.

Typical mistake

It is an error to see multiculturalism as an ideology. While a harmonious, multicultural society may be a goal of many social reformers, it does not envisage a single view of how society should be organised, as ideologies do, but rather that society should be based on a collection of values that embodies tolerance and a celebration of diversity.

Core ideas of multiculturalism

Human nature

REVISED

Conceptions of human nature are fundamental to multiculturalism. Those who advocate multiculturalism typically hold the following views about human nature.

Community spirit

- They see ourselves as part of a community rather than as individuals. This is often described as **communitarianism**.
- Optimistically, human nature tends towards **tolerance**, sympathy and empathy with fellow humans rather than towards competitiveness and antagonism.
- Humans have a malleable, flexible nature. Like anarchists and many socialists, those who support multiculturalism believe that we are the products of the society in which we live. Thus, if we live in a diverse but harmonious society, we will come to tolerate and celebrate diversity.
- This has been described as an embedded sense of communalism in that it becomes fundamental to our existence.

Communitarianism People see themselves in terms of the multiple communities of which they are a part. These may be based on such elements as religion, culture or ethnicity.

Tolerance Idea associated with the origins of liberalism in the eighteenth century. Such liberals saw different beliefs and lifestyles as having equal value, so they should be tolerated and equally respected. By introducing tolerance, diversity in society can be encouraged and become a positive force.

Identity

- The concept of **identity politics** is widely respected in society and means that individuals regard the existence of separate identities as natural. This has been described by the Canadian sociologist Charles Taylor as the **'politics of recognition'**.
- In contrast to liberals, who see identity in terms of self-realisation, the multicultural outlook sees identity in terms of our relationships with other individuals and groups.
- We understand our own identity in terms of both the communities to which we belong and the different communities to which we do not belong. This is an idea also largely associated with Charles Taylor.
- The existence of a very diverse society helps individuals to understand identity and does not, as opponents of multiculturalism suggest, confuse our sense of identity.

> **Identity politics** A belief and aspiration that states and their policy makers should see individuals in terms of their multiple identities and should take into account diversity rather than seek to suppress it.

Recognition of identity

- Members of society should recognise the existence of diverse identities.
- Recognition of different identities requires that those different identities be respected.
- Different communities must develop self-respect in order to learn how to recognise and respect other identities in a society.

Key thinker

Charles Taylor (1931–)

Taylor is a Canadian liberal.

The main ideas of Charles Taylor are as follows:
- His views are often described as communitarianism.
- Communitarianism suggests that humankind is fundamentally social and that we see our identity more in terms of our community than as individuals.

- Our sense of identity derives from our relationships with social groups such as the family, religions, occupations and pastimes.
- Politics tends to stress the idea of a 'national culture' while humans actually view their identities in terms of smaller, specialised communities.
- States and their policy makers should take into account diverse identities.

Essentialism

- In each community within society, members necessarily share a number of essential values.
- This suggests that human nature directs that we will always share the common values of our original community, even if we leave that community and become part of wider society.
- The **essentialist** nature of our cultural identity should be recognised. Attempts to suppress its values and practices will be unlikely to succeed.

> **Essentialism** Different communities contain characteristics which mean that their values will be deeply entrenched. This entrenched nature of cultural, ethnic or gender identities means that there will always be a strong sense of cohesion within the various communities.

Society

REVISED

Unlike liberals, multicultural thinkers believe that the concept of society is vital. They reject the classical liberal and neo-liberal view that we are essentially individuals with purely individual goals. The relationship between multiculturalism and society includes the following elements.

Exam practice answers and quick quizzes at
www.hoddereducation.co.uk/myrevisionnotesdownloads

The importance of society

- We see ourselves as members of a society rather than as pure individuals. Social progress is threatened by excessive individualism.
- Society is made up more of communities than of individuals.
- Society, and the communities within it, shapes us as individuals rather than the other way round.

Communities

- Though there are geographical communities (villages, towns, regions, cities, etc.) which are important, they are not what multicultural thinkers mean by 'community'.
- For multicultural thinkers, a community is defined as a group of people who have shared beliefs, lifestyles, aspirations and activities.
- Communities often have very specific historical origins. These may be rooted in such factors as ethnicity, religion, gender and sexual orientation.
- When a community has both a cultural and a geographical identity (e.g. Asian communities in specific city districts), it is the common cultural identity that is important rather than the geographical identity.

Diversity

- The increasing diversity of modern societies — the UK being a prime example — is seen as a positive development.
- The existence of diversity can be directed towards positive goals such as greater tolerance, economic progress and cultural development.
- The more people become aware of the nature of different cultures, through the growth of diverse societies, the more they develop tolerance and understanding. Diversity does not, as opponents of multiculturalism suggest, breed antagonism.
- Celebration of diversity insists that no culture is superior or inferior to any other. This implies that there is no such thing as a single conception of what is meant by the term 'the good life'.
- Tariq Modood calls a diverse society imbued with tolerance and mutual understanding a **'community of communities'**.

The state

REVISED

The ways in which a state reacts to multiculturalism are crucial to how it is likely to develop. Various reactions can be identified.

Assimilation

- Assimilation is a reaction against the process of multiculturalism.
- In essence, assimilation is a policy which seeks to ensure that different groups are absorbed into the dominant **culture** of a society.
- Institutions that tend to encourage separate identities may be suppressed. Schools are a special target, with faith schools being suppressed or possibly even made illegal.
- There may be suppression of practices that emphasise cultural difference, such as distinctive clothing like Muslim veils.

Segregation

- One answer to problems relating to multicultural societies is to promote **segregation** between communities.

Culture A term relating to the dominant values, beliefs, heritage and lifestyle of a particular community.

Segregation A situation where the diversity of different communities has led to separation rather than integration. As such communities develop defensive attitudes, they become increasingly geographically segregated.

- Segregation implies various measures to keep communities apart, geographically and culturally. This may mean separate education for different cultures, for instance. Northern Ireland has been an example of this.
- Segregation may also imply the introduction of **differential rights,** whereby various ethnic and religious groups are granted separate rights.

> **Differential rights** In opposition to value pluralism, this idea suggests that values are of different worth and the state should respect the fact that some minority communities value some rights above others. For example, Muslims may value individual liberty below religious commandments. Members of orthodox religious communities may not observe tolerance towards liberal versions of their religion.

Integration

- Integration acknowledges the need for individuals whose culture is not the dominant culture of a society to be able to pursue their beliefs and lifestyle.
- The idea of **value pluralism** means that all groups in society have a clear set of values which they are expected to practise and/or respect.
- However, the integration approach to policy insists that there are certain dominant, fundamental laws and practices that must be adhered to. This follows the liberal belief that there is a basic difference between private life and public life. Cultural differences should be tolerated in private life but not in public life. For example, Rastafarians may follow their own religious beliefs but the smoking of cannabis, which is part of their culture, is a public activity and thus remains illegal in the UK.
- Integrationists support legal protection for minority cultures provided they do not commit public offences.

The multiculturalist state

The pure multicultural state will exhibit the following characteristics:

- The legal practices of minority communities are tolerated and even protected by the state.
- There will be **formal equality**, in that all individuals and communities enjoy equal civil rights.
- There should be a high degree of **multicultural integration**.
- Minority languages are respected and provision is made for their place in education.
- Education also recognises the existence of various minority communities and teaches tolerance and understanding.
- The values that the state recognises as fundamental to society are recognised and respected by all minority communities. This idea has its origins in the work of liberal philosopher Isaiah Berlin.
- Discrimination against minorities is outlawed.
- The legal system of the state makes allowances for laws practised by minority communities (such as Sharia law) to co-exist with national laws provided there is no conflict between them.
- A degree of **positive discrimination** is practised by the state to counteract discriminatory practices against minorities.
- Bodies that represent the interests of minority groups, such as a Muslim parliament or other religious assemblies, should be supported by the central state.

Value pluralism Relates to the philosopher Isaiah Berlin, who argued that in liberal-based societies there are a number of fundamental values which the state should recognise and foster. These include tolerance, equal rights, individual liberty and mutual respect. These values are of equal worth.

Formal equality A situation where the state imposes legal equality for all individuals and groups in society. It is also described as 'equal rights'.

Multicultural integration The idea that even in culturally and racially diverse communities, there can be a strong degree of integration, leading to social harmony.

Positive discrimination A practice designed to combat negative discrimination. Where minority groups, or women, find themselves suffering discrimination in fields such as employment, business, politics and education, the state may create legal assurances to give a positive advantage to such groups in order to create more equality of outcome. It may also involve creating 'quotas' to ensure such groups are awarded greater opportunities for advancement.

Exam practice answers and quick quizzes at www.hoddereducation.co.uk/myrevisionnotesdownloads

Now test yourself

1 What is being described in each of these cases?
   (a) A principle that all communities should have the same civil rights.
   (b) The anti-multiculturalist idea that all minority communities should be absorbed into the national community.
   (c) The idea that all groups in a society have their own value systems which they adhere to.
   (d) A phenomenon whereby different cultural groups in society tend to be kept separate in order to avoid conflict.

Answers on p. 111

The economy

The general principle here is that economic policies and structures should ensure that all groups in society have their economic needs attended to and have equal access to economic opportunities. The following elements are important.

Capitalism and multiculturalism

- Most multiculturalists see free-market capitalism as an aid to the economic development of various minority groups.
- Cosmopolitan integration sees globalisation as a positive development for various cultures. The peripatetic nature of globalised economies provides opportunities for migrant groups.
- States nevertheless must recognise that free-market capitalism creates inequality and that some communities may suffer disproportionately from such inequality. Therefore steps need to be taken to recognise and counteract such developments.

Socialism and multiculturalism

- Socialists suggest that the inequality caused by free-market capitalism tends to affect minority cultures disproportionately.
- To some extent this can be combatted by positive discrimination and by formal equality.
- Economic policies designed to combat inequality must also include recognition of the special problems encountered by minority communities.

> **Exam tip**
>
> Be very careful how you use the terms 'values', 'culture' and 'community'.
> - **Values** are firmly held ideas about our attitudes and how we should live our life, including such concepts as tolerance, justice, freedom and equality.
> - **Culture** refers to the traditions, belief systems and common practices of a community, such as religion, attitudes to gender relations, customs and internal legal systems such as Sharia law.
> - **Community** refers to any group that separates itself and makes itself distinctive in any way. Communities may be based on such distinctions as religion, ethnicity, sexual orientation or ideology.

> **Typical mistake**
>
> It is common to confuse the terms 'society' and 'community'. Society refers to the whole population of a country or a distinct region of a country. Community refers to some part of a society that considers itself distinctive to a greater or lesser extent.

Different types of multiculturalism

Liberal multiculturalism

Positive links

- The most fundamental form of liberal multiculturalism takes the 'modern' liberal view that freedom is about self-determination and self-realisation.
- All liberals accept the principle that tolerance is a fundamental virtue. In accordance with J.S. Mill's 'harm principle', liberal multiculturalists believe that all forms of activity, belief and lifestyle should be tolerated as long as they do no harm to others. Will Kymlicka widens this to suggest there are universal social values applicable in all circumstances.
- An additional liberal idea is that society and the state should offer **group differential rights**, where feasible, whereby some groups may have separate rights of their own, as long as the exercise of these rights does no harm to others and does not interfere with the rights of other groups.
- Most liberals accept that diversity in society is something to be celebrated as well as protected.
- Liberals believe that cultural diversity is a positive force, creating economic and cultural development.
- Classical liberals of the nineteenth century believed that liberty and democracy were 'developmental' in that they promote the advancement of individuals. To this, modern liberals add cultural diversity.
- Modern liberals generally reject direct democracy, on the grounds that it represents the 'tyranny of the majority'. They insist democracy must take account of the interests of cultural minorities.

> **Group differential rights**
> Rights that might be granted to some groups even though they are not universally applied. In their most extreme form such rights may allow a group to be self-governing.

Key thinker

Will Kymlicka (1962–)

Like Charles Taylor, Kymlicka is Canadian. The reason for Canadian interest in multiculturalism is that there is a long history in that country of controversy over whether the French-speaking minority in Quebec should be allowed to retain a separate identity or should be integrated into wider Canadian society.

The main ideas of Will Kymlicka are as follows:
- He is fundamentally a modern liberal.
- He believes that fundamental liberal principles are applicable in all societies and communities at all times.

- He sees an individual's attachment to a particular culture and to its characteristics as a positive force, in particular that it is an aid to individualism. It does not, he asserts, suppress individualism. He refers to qualities such as **'self-confidence'** and **'self-fulfilment'** arising from strong cultural identity.
- Cultural choice is important. In a mono-cultural society, choices are too limited.
- He developed the idea of group differential rights, whereby cultural groups might be granted rights separate from those enjoyed by society in general. When such rights are granted, members of minority groups are more likely, not less likely, to become **'good citizens'**.

> **Typical mistake**
>
> Multiculturalism should not be seen as a purely 'liberal' set of beliefs. Conservatives and socialists can also support multiculturalism, and there are some ways in which liberalism and multiculturalism may be seen to be in opposition to each other.

Exam practice answers and quick quizzes at
www.hoddereducation.co.uk/myrevisionnotesdownloads

Negative links

There are several ways in which it could be said that there are contradictions between liberalism and multiculturalism (see Table 7.1). Among them are these:

- Liberalism is a doctrine of freedom and individualism; multicultural thinkers tend to stress membership of a community. It could be argued that the stress on community is a denial of individualism — it denies that we are all individuals with individual identities.
- Many cultural communities, especially religions, preach values which are at odds with liberalism, notably lack of tolerance, discrimination against women and suppression of free thinking. This leads to the conundrum: 'should liberals tolerate intolerant belief systems?'
- Many communities are fundamentally conservative in nature, so liberal values are alien to them.
- Liberalism is a rational ideology whereas many communities are based on religion, emotional attachments or spirituality and can be seen as denials of rationalism.

Table 7.1 Links and contradictions between liberalism and multiculturalism

Links	Contradictions
Tolerance is a key element of liberalism and is essential for a successful multicultural society.	Some cultural and religious communities are fundamentally intolerant of alternative belief systems and practices.
Multiculturalist liberals claim that a multicultural society encourages individualism and individual self-realisation.	The multiculturalist stress on the idea of 'community' and collective membership of communities may be seen as a denial of individualism.
Liberalism suggests that there are a number of values which are fundamental to all societies at all times. This may be described as 'absolute morality'.	Multiculturalism suggests that there can be a degree of 'moral relativism'. This suggests that some communities may have value systems which contradict liberal values and these can be tolerated.
Liberals see all basic values as having equal value.	Some minority communities grant different values to various beliefs and principles.
A number of principles sacred to modern liberalism, such as equal rights, anti-discrimination, democracy and religious freedom, can be imposed throughout society if there is 'real' multiculturalism because a distinction can be drawn between private morality and public morality.	Some communities do not accept the distinction between private and public morality and so reserve the right to offend liberal principles even if they are widely accepted in a society.

Key thinker

Isaiah Berlin (1909–97)

Berlin was one of the most prominent twentieth-century liberal philosophers in the western world. His analysis of liberalism is widely accepted as the ultimate expression of the ideology.

The main ideas of Isaiah Berlin were as follows:
- He was fundamentally a modern liberal.
- He developed the idea of **'moral pluralism'**, which asserts that there are some moral values that are common to all communities, such

as liberty, equality and honesty, while there are other moral values that vary from one community to another.
- Sometimes, Berlin acknowledged, one of the absolute values might conflict with another (equality can conflict with freedom, tolerance can conflict with justice). This would not be a problem if these values were ranked in importance, but they are not. Because they are of equal worth, it is not possible to determine which should prevail.

- As a liberal, Berlin rejected the idea that the state should resolve such conflicts through the law (that would be dictatorial and undemocratic).
- He therefore argued that it is up to each individual community to resolve these conflicts in its own way. He called this value pluralism.
- Berlin rejected the practice of some communities to 'trap' their members. He argued that people must be free to leave one community and join another.

Typical mistake

Berlin pre-dates the concept of multiculturalism so he must never be described as an advocate of multiculturalism. It is better to assert that his ideas have been adapted by modern multicultural thinkers.

Exam tip

As with all the examined political ideas, it is vital to quote some of the key thinkers when discussing ideas and debates.

Pluralist multiculturalism

REVISED

This philosophy is associated with Bhikhu Parekh, a British politician in the Labour Party. The main ideas of pluralist multiculturalism include the following:

- It recognises the globalised nature of the modern world.
- There are many different value systems flourishing in the world, some of them religious, others political or ideological, and some nationalistic or tribal in nature.
- Attempting to impose liberal values on these groups is futile.
- It is therefore important that states and their policy makers should acknowledge this.
- Attempting to impose liberal values on the pluralism of world value systems is likely to cause excessive conflict.
- Pluralist multiculturalism has also influenced members of the socialist left.
- Some socialists argue that contesting value systems and cultures should receive economic protection and may even receive state subsidies.

Key thinker

Bhikhu Parekh (1935–)

Parekh is a Labour peer who sits in the House of Lords and stands at the left extreme of the multiculturalist movement.

The main ideas of Bhikhu Parekh are as follows:
- While most liberals propose what is called 'shallow diversity', Parekh's ideas are often described as 'deep diversity' (see Table 7.2).
- His ideas have been described as a 'community of communities'.
- Parekh believes that attempts to create a single value system in a society to which all cultures can subscribe are doomed to failure at best and may cause social conflict at worst.
- He has argued that different legal systems can co-exist. For example, Islamic Sharia law can, within some restrictions, co-exist with UK national law.
- Parekh argues that it is perfectly possible for an individual to be a loyal citizen of the state as well as being committed to a separate cultural identity.
- Every culture has its strengths and weaknesses and the state should recognise this.

Exam practice answers and quick quizzes at
www.hoddereducation.co.uk/myrevisionnotesdownloads

Table 7.2 Deep diversity versus shallow diversity

Deep diversity	Shallow diversity
Associated with key thinkers Bhikhu Parekh and Charles Taylor.	Associated with key thinkers such as Will Kymlicka and Tariq Modood.
There should be equal treatment and respect for the values of all communities within a society. This may include altering national laws to accommodate minority practices, an idea known as **individualist integration**.	The national values of the dominant culture should be seen as non-negotiable, while minority cultures must conform to the national culture.
Deep diversity supports identity politics, which suggests that an individual's identity is shaped by the community in which they live rather than by society as a whole.	Shallow diversity implies that **universalism** is important. That is the principle that there are social values which should be fundamental to all societies and communities, no matter what separate identities individuals may adopt for themselves.
Laws and practices adopted by minority communities should be allowed to co-exist alongside national laws as far as possible.	Laws and practices of minority cultures must conform to national law.
Diverse cultural developments should be encouraged and not suppressed.	While diverse cultures are to be tolerated and celebrated, there remains a stress on national values.
The key to social cohesion and harmony is dialogue between different cultures. This can be described as 'dynamic multiculturalism' in that diversity will take from the strengths of all cultures and the weaknesses will be marginalised.	It is the role of the state to promote social harmony. Diversity of cultures enriches society and this development should be state-led.

Individualist integration Where the state recognises that some allowances in the law can and should be made to accommodate cultural differences. This may involve exemptions from some law on the grounds of belief, such as exemptions from Christian worship in schools for members of other faiths.

Universalism The idea, associated with multiculturalism (notably shallow diversity), that there are some social values that can and should be applied to all societies, whatever their belief system or heritage. For example, the idea of tolerance should be universally applied even when a belief system is not intrinsically tolerant of others.

TESTED

Now test yourself

2 State whether you think the following ideas are examples of 'shallow' or 'deep' diversity.
  (a) The observance of specific minority community values places a stress on national values and so should be de-emphasised.
  (b) The national values of a society should not be compromised by minority value systems.
  (c) There should be equal treatment and respect for all minority value systems in a society.
  (d) Legal systems used within minority communities should be allowed to co-exist alongside national laws.

Answers on p. 111

Cosmopolitan multiculturalism

Fundamentally, cosmopolitan multiculturalism sees people very much as individuals. It denies that we are destined to remain part of one culture all our lives. In the modern globalised world, many cultures co-exist and each individual state must acknowledge that fact. The main principles of cosmopolitan multiculturalism include the following:

- The idea of **cosmopolitan integration** suggests that the world consists of many different communities and cultures, and that individuals may choose which culture they belong to.
- Many individuals may see themselves as members of more than one cultural community.
- It is implied that attachments to cultural communities should generally be weak so that there are few, if any, contradictions between an individual's membership of different cultures. Thus, one may be Asian, a member of a church and gay without any contradictions between them.
- The switching of people from one culture to another is sometimes described as 'cultural tourism'.

> **Cosmopolitan integration**
> The idea that integration should not be confined to a single society or state but should exist on a worldwide basis. This implies that tolerance and mutual respect should be universal. It also suggests that individuals may choose which cultural community to join and may see themselves as members of several communities.

Key thinker

Tariq Modood (1952–)

Modood is a British-Asian academic who has acted as an adviser to UK governments on issues concerning racial integration and multiculturalism.

The main ideas of Tariq Modood are as follows:

- His main concern is the nature of a multiracial society and the role of the state in creating such a situation.
- His ideas have been described as 'unity through diversity'.
- His fundamental philosophy is that a successfully diverse society can promote unity rather than disunity.
- By stressing the strengths of various cultural identities, society can be enriched. This may be achieved through, for example, faith schools, state support for community groups and legal protection for faith and ethnic groups.
- Modood has stressed that cultural diversity and tolerance of various cultures have become part of dominant British culture. Indeed, British culture can be seen as 'superior' on the grounds of such diversity.
- The strength of British society is that there are now so many separate local communities which foster a sense of dynamism and dynamic individualism.
- Modood has sometimes been described as a conservative multiculturalist in that his ideas are similar to David Cameron's Big Society concept, where a multiplicity of small local groups can achieve social progress through local action.

Now test yourself

3 What aspect of multiculturalism is being described in each case?
  (a) The idea that integration should not be confined to a single society or state but should exist on a worldwide basis.
  (b) The idea that there are some values that should be applied to all societies, at all times and in any circumstances.
  (c) The practice of giving an artificial advantage to one minority group, or to women, over others in the fields of applying for employment, applying for educational opportunities and applying for political positions.
  (d) A single word referring to the dominant practices, beliefs, customs and traditions of a particular community.

Answers on p. 111

Exam practice answers and quick quizzes at
www.hoddereducation.co.uk/myrevisionnotesdownloads

Multiculturalism and conservatism

The key links (positive and negative) between multiculturalism and conservatism include these.

Negative

- Excessive cultural diversity is seen by many conservatives as a threat to the organic society and to social cohesion.
- Conservatives generally celebrate traditions. Cultural diversity may threaten adherence to a country's cherished traditions.
- In so far as multiculturalism requires state intervention, conservatives fear that an interfering state will become too powerful and overbearing.

Positive

- An important conservative principle is 'reform in order to conserve'. This implies that reforms which recognise cultural diversity and extract positive elements from it will conserve society and prevent rather than promote disharmony.
- For many conservatives, the multicultural society has now become part of Britain's post-colonial character. It has also been woven into our traditions, so there is no contradiction between multiculturalism and respect for tradition.
- There is a strong conservative traditional belief, ranging from Edmund Burke in the late eighteenth century to David Cameron recently, that strong, active local communities (which Burke called **'little platoons'**) are key social phenomena. Many such communities are based on minority cultures, so multiculturalism can be a positive force.

> **Typical mistake**
>
> Just as it is a mistake to assume that multiculturalism is merely a branch of liberalism, it is also wrong to believe that all conservatives are anti-multiculturalism (though some populist, right-wing conservatives are); rather, conservatives tend to stress a different kind of multiculturalism.

Multiculturalism and socialism

The key links (negative and positive) between multiculturalism and socialism include these.

Negative

- Fundamentalist socialists see the multicultural debate as a distraction from the true nature of economic inequality and oppression. They still stress class conflicts and see racial and inter-community tensions as mere reflections of class conflict.
- Socialists have criticised some minority communities, usually religious groups, on the grounds that they create their own internal forms of exploitation, for example of women or of members of a lower caste. This leads to a socialist argument that such practices need to be suppressed.
- Some socialists have argued that positive measures to improve the economic position of some minority groups undermine the fundamental socialist goal of achieving a national-based form of 'just society'.

Positive

- Socialists are instinctively drawn towards the promotion of equal rights. This applies both to individuals and to whole minority communities.

- Some minority communities, notably Muslims in the UK, suffer from persistent economic deprivation and lack of opportunity. Socialist-style interventions can assist in creating more equality between communities and so breed greater harmony.
- Socialists recognise that there is great inequality between the 'majority' community and 'minority' communities, creating social tension. By shifting resources and wealth generally from the majority to minorities, greater mutual respect can be achieved.
- Many socialists equate economic exploitation with racism. Thus, by reducing such exploitation, racism can also be reduced. Socialists therefore propose measures to create equality of opportunity and positive discrimination.

Table 7.3 outlines multiculturalist tendencies.

Table 7.3 Three multiculturalist tendencies

Liberal	Conservative	Socialist
People see themselves in terms of their membership of communities as well as being individuals pursuing self-interest.	Multiculturalism and the acceptance of diversity threaten the cohesion of an organic society.	Multiculturalism should be confined to creating greater economic equality in society.
The values of minority communities should be respected in the same way that national values are respected.	Minority values often threaten national values and traditions and therefore must be seen as inferior and sometimes even subversive.	Minority values and practices should be tolerated only if they do not lead to the economic exploitation of certain groups.
Most liberals tolerate identity politics, arguing that people may have multiple cultural identities.	Members of minority communities should consider their identification with the state and the wider nation as more important than their own separate community identity.	Though separate community identities are inevitable, people should primarily view their identity in terms of their position within the class system.
The state has a positive role to play in creating greater understanding between communities, as well as mutual respect and tolerance.	While many conservatives support the aims of multiculturalism, they are suspicious of excessive state intervention to achieve such goals.	Intervention by the state is needed if there is excessive economic inequality and exploitation either of minority communities by the majority culture or within such communities.

Now test yourself

TESTED ☐

4 Identify the key thinker being described in each case.
   (a) A twentieth-century liberal philosopher who developed the idea of moral pluralism, suggesting some moral values are common to all societies.
   (b) A British-Pakistani social theorist who argued that cultural diversity was a positive force, suggesting it brought 'unity through diversity'.
   (c) A Canadian multiculturalist who developed the idea of 'communitarianism'.
   (d) A British multicultural thinker whose ideas are often described as 'deep diversity'.

Answers on p. 111

Exam tip

Make sure you are able to distinguish between typical liberal, conservative and socialist perspectives on multiculturalism as many questions will require a knowledge of such distinctions.

Exam practice answers and quick quizzes at
www.hoddereducation.co.uk/myrevisionnotesdownloads

Tensions within multiculturalism

Although multiculturalism has been seen as a single movement, this is something of an illusion: there remain serious divisions within it. Four dominant tensions can be identified. These are shown in Table 7.4.

Table 7.4 Tensions within multiculturalism

Tendency	Counter-tendency
Pluralist multiculturalists such as Parekh see people as mainly concerned with the interests of their own communities.	Liberal and cosmopolitan multiculturalists see people as individuals pursuing self-interest.
The pluralist model suggests there should be social equality within communities.	Liberal multiculturalists accept that individual progress is dependent on their own efforts so that inequality is inevitable.
Shallow diversity suggests the state should seek to promote or even impose the core values of a society upon all communities.	Deep diversity supports 'cultural federalism' where various cultures are encouraged by the state and may co-exist alongside the dominant culture.
Liberal multiculturalists on the whole support free trade and the free movement of both goods and people, with little or no state intervention to reduce inequality.	Pluralist multiculturalists accept that some communities may need some degree of 'socialist'-style intervention in order to address institutional inequality, from which they may suffer persistently.

Multiculturalism today

Multiculturalism today faces a number of challenges. Among them are these:

- The huge movements of people who are refugees, asylum seekers and economic migrants into established modern liberal democracies have placed significant strains on the dominant cultures and the value systems of the receiving countries as well as creating social and political discord.
- There has been a rise in the popularity and electability of right-wing populist parties opposed to multiculturalism, such as America First, UKIP and Five Star in Italy.
- Conservative politicians and parties have been challenging multiculturalism by stressing the need for social integration and assimilation so that cultural differences are eroded rather than being viewed positively. This has occurred in western society through the banning of some overt religious practices (France) and attacks on the exclusivity of many faith schools (the UK).
- The rise of jihadist extremism has created tendencies which militate against multiculturalism and in favour of the suppression of religious cultures and values.
- Multiculturalism has been blamed, especially in the UK, for the increasing 'ghettoisation' of some groups in towns and cities. Conservatives argue that excessive toleration of separate cultures encourages members of such minorities to group themselves together into exclusive communities, thus challenging the multicultural support for mutual dialogue, understanding and respect between cultures. This has been described as segregation rather than integration.
- Nevertheless, multiculturalism remains a powerful force in liberal-based societies and is now seen as one of the key weapons against the rise of right-wing populism.

Exam practice

You must use appropriate thinkers you have studied to support your answer and consider both sides in a balanced way.

1 To what extent is multiculturalism a purely liberal idea?   [24]
2 To what extent is multiculturalism incompatible with conservatism?   [24]
3 To what extent is multiculturalism a denial of identity politics?   [24]

Answers and quick quiz 7 online

ONLINE

Summary

You should now have an understanding of:

- the distinction between liberal, socialist and conservative perspectives on multiculturalism
- the implications of integration and assimilation
- the nature of cosmopolitan integration
- the various reasons why multiculturalism has been criticised
- the ways in which the state can promote multiculturalism

- the relationship between the core values of societies and minority values, including the distinctions between public and private values
- the tensions that exist within the multiculturalist movement
- how multiculturalism has been challenged and actually blamed, in some cases, for inter-community tensions.

8 Ecologism

The origins of ecologism

Ernst Haeckel coined the term 'ecology' in 1879 as a study of the relationship between living organisms and their organic and non-organic environment. Ecologism cannot be described as a coherent movement as there is diversity in both its objectives and its goals. However, it does have some common values, primarily that the non-human world deserves and demands central consideration within the organisation of state (nationally and internationally), society and economy.

- The term 'shallow green' was originally coined by Arne Naess in 1972 as a criticism of the anthropocentric nature of this branch of ecology.
- **Anthropocentrism** has its origins in Abrahamic religions where God gave the human race dominion over the environment.
- Rationalists from the Enlightenment perceived humans as above nature. John Locke argued, **'We are the masters and possessors of nature.'** In the industrial era, nature became subservient to human economic and materialistic needs.
- Deep green ecologists argue for **ecocentrism**. They maintain that the 'enlightened anthropocentrism' adopted by shallow green ecologists is doomed to fail as the need to dominate nature is too ingrained in the human psyche.
- Social ecologists argue that environmental degradation is linked to specific social constructs that must be overturned before radical ecological change can occur. Murray Bookchin coined the term **'social ecology'** and there are three separate branches: eco-anarchism, ecosocialism and ecofeminism.

> **Anthropocentrism**
> The idea that human interests are of primary importance, which is the opposite of ecocentrism. Shallow green ecologists argue for 'enlightened anthropocentrism' whereby humans act like stewards of the environment, protecting the natural world so that it can continue to support human life.
>
> **Ecocentrism** A nature-centred rather than a human-centred system of values. It therefore gives priority to ecological balance over human wants and needs.

> **Exam tip**
>
> Ecology is the only political idea that challenges the supremacy of human interest, as it argues, to differing degrees, for the primacy of nature and the interdependency of all life forms with their environment.

Core ideas of ecologism

Human nature

REVISED

- Shallow green ecologists argue that humans are anthropocentric primarily due to the long-standing influence of Abrahamic religions such Judaism, Christianity and Islam, which claim that God created the planet for humankind to 'rule over'.
- Rachel Carson argued that humans have been exploiting the environment for so long that they are oblivious to the damage they are causing.
- Shallow green ecologists say that human nature must become one of enlightened anthropocentrism, where we recognise our environmental responsibility and act as responsible stewards.

- The development of an **environmental consciousness** is needed so that humans can identify with the non-human world. This will result in a radical change in both human nature and society, leading to new environmental ethics.
- Shallow green ecologists perceive these environmental ethics as underpinning state, society and economy. Humans would adopt weak **sustainability**; nation-states would adopt managerialism to regulate environmental problems, such as encouraging **biodiversity**, preserving natural resources, energy conservation, recycling, and strict control over both atmospheric and water pollution.
- Deep green ecologists disagree with anthropocentrism, so they define environmental consciousness as placing itself within the natural world and not as distinct from it.
- Deep green ecologists argue that there needs to be a revolutionary change to create an ecocentric environmental consciousness with more radical environmental ethics. This has been influenced by Zen Buddhism, which preaches the unity of all things.
- Aldo Leopold argued for environmental ethics that recognised strong sustainability and **biocentric equality** where 'soils, waters, plants and animals' have an intrinsic value rather than having their utility measured simply by their worth to humans.
- Social ecologists argue that there needs to be a radical social change before an environmental consciousness is possible. Eco-anarchism and ecosocialism both require communist economic systems while ecofeminists require the overthrow of patriarchy.

Key thinker

Aldo Leopold (1887–1948)

Leopold was a pioneer of early ecologistic thought, whose ideas later influenced deep green thinking.

The main ideas of Aldo Leopold were as follows:
- The land ethic: humans should accept that the land, which incorporates **'soils, waters, plants and animals'**, does not belong to them. There should be biocentric equality where all beings and the community have equal value.
- Conservation fails because it is based on an economic model where land is valued merely as a commodity of monetary worth.
- Human nature must alter to a new environmental consciousness so that land and nature are no longer perceived as resources to be exploited. The new environmental ethics would be that land would not be seen as a commodity; humans would perceive nature as a holistic community. The land would be respected for its intrinsic value rather than its monetary worth.
- Biodiversity is therefore essential to conserve endangered species and their habitats.
- This is also the case for the concept of 'wilderness': landscapes free from human interference preserved in their natural state.
- Leopold pioneered a spiritual relationship with the land that influenced later ecological thinkers such as Arne Naess.

Environmental consciousness A state of being where humans' sense of self is fully realised by a deep identification with the non-human world. This consciousness will be the basis for a new foundation of environmental ethics and social organisation.

Sustainability The capacity of the ecological system to maintain its health over time. Deep green ecologists argue for strong sustainability, which would radically alter human activity by opposing economic growth and materialism, enabling society to shift to self-contained small communities. Shallow green ecologists argue for weak sustainability, which is reformist and proposes more environmentally sound capitalism.

Biodiversity The belief that as many species of plants and animals must survive and flourish as possible to maintain a richness of nature. This will bring health and stability to the broad eco-community.

Biocentric equality The radical idea that all human beings within the biotic community have equal intrinsic value. This is radical as it contradicts conventional anthropocentric society.

> **Exam tip**
>
> Ecologism has multiple definitions for environmental consciousness and environmental ethics. These concepts can be both reformist and radical. Give examples from the key thinkers to corroborate your points.

Exam practice answers and quick quizzes at
www.hoddereducation.co.uk/myrevisionnotesdownloads

Key thinker

Rachel Carson (1907–64)

Carson's influential book *The Silent Spring* (1962) was one of the early works that brought the science of ecology to public attention for the first time.

The main ideas of Rachel Carson were as follows:
- State and society do not have the authority to dominate nature — **'the gods of profit and production'**, i.e. big business and the state, were putting economic concerns above ecological issues, which was having a destructive effect on nature.
- *The Silent Spring* gave examples of the damage to rivers, lakes, fauna and flora from the use of the pesticide DDT.
- Pollution, particularly of the water supply, will eventually threaten humans' health.
- Nature should be seen holistically — humans are not superior to nature and they need to develop a holistic, enlightened, anthropocentric consciousness concerning the interconnectedness of nature. Nature does not exist for humans' convenience.
- Agricultural production with no thought of the wider negative consequences for flora and fauna will be disastrous in the long run.
- Although Carson advised the US government on some of the first legal environmental limits on polluting, she never offered a detailed ecological strategy to tackle the problems she had highlighted.

The state

REVISED

- Ecologism has contradictory views on the role of the state, which are both positive and negative.
- Some shallow green ecologists argue for weak sustainability and managerialism where the state intervenes at the national and international level to regulate environmental problems. Examples include the UN Framework Convention on Climate Change, the Intergovernmental Panel on Climate Change (IPCC), the UK Climate Change Act 2008 and the Paris accord of 2015.
- Other shallow green ecologists argue for more free-market solutions, such as green capitalism to incentivise good behaviour via the market. Examples include Nestlé's zero deforestation policy.
- Shallow green ecologists retain the post-Enlightenment mechanistic world view that nature is like a machine that can be understood, fixed or replaced in isolation. The state's faith in technological solutions such as carbon-capture technology to control climate change is an example of this.
- Key thinkers Rachel Carson and Aldo Leopold both view the state as having a role to protect the environment.
- Deep green ecologists are conflicted on the role of the state:
  ○ E.F. Schumacher argues that the state is overbearing and therefore should be decentralised, which will result in localism, pastoralism and strong sustainability.
  ○ Murray Bookchin argues that the state must be abolished as it is an enemy of both liberty and nature. Bookchin envisaged a society of small communities based on shared property and strong sustainability.
- Social ecologists are also conflicted over the role of the state:
  ○ Eco-anarchists and ecosocialists view the state as enforcing capitalism and **industrialism**. It will therefore need to be abolished so that society can be communist in nature.
  ○ Ecofeminists argue that the state reinforces patriarchy. Following a societal transformation, the state, embracing feminine values, will be nurturing rather than exploitative in nature.

Industrialism Based on large-scale production and a faith in science and technology to deliver limitless growth to satisfy material needs.

Key thinker

Murray Bookchin (1921–2006)

Bookchin is famous for coining the phrase **'social ecology'** and offering an eco-anarchistic view of society that was both anti-capitalistic and pro-decentralisation.

The main ideas of Murray Bookchin were as follows:
- The environmental crisis emerges from existing social structures of oppression.
- Ecological destruction is the consequence of human social structures and the need to dominate society, also resulting in war, racism, sexism and exploitation of the third world.
- Underpinning this need to dominate is another social structure: the devotion to capitalism. The environment is consumed, damaged and destroyed by capitalism's compulsion for materialism, consumerism and economic growth.
- Bookchin argues that hierarchies, inherent in human state and society, facilitate the domination.
- Shallow green ecology and anthropocentrism are flawed as capitalism's *raison d'être* is continuous economic growth, which always supersedes environmental concerns.

Therefore, lessons should be learned from ecology:
- A new society — **'ecotopia'** — is needed to replace traditional capitalistic society.

- This revolutionary approach would be anarchist in nature — no state — based on commonly owned, small communities run with an egalitarian ethos.
- This **'anarcho-communism'** would establish new environmental ethics, abolishing private property and redistributing wealth according to need. Society would no longer be about industrialism's unsustainable pursuit of economic growth; rather, society would become non-capitalist.
- These environmental ethics would lead to a new environmental consciousness that would be strictly rational in nature. Bookchin distrusted deep green thinkers who argued for a Zen Buddhist component to environmental consciousness, dismissing it as **'eco-la-la'**.
- Most importantly, hierarchy, which facilitates dominating human behaviour, would be replaced by direct democracy with communal decision making and **decentralisation**.
- Replacing capitalism would end the unsustainable consumption of resources, which would negate ecological degradation.
- Ecotopia would create a new rational environmental consciousness where humans would live in harmony with nature rather than trying to dominate it. It is therefore ecocentric.

Exam tip

Ecotopia is a word that combines the word 'ecology' with 'utopia', which means a perfect society. In creating this new word, Bookchin was trying to say that the perfect society was an ecological society.

Typical mistake

Students often describe Bookchin as ecocentric, which is a simplification. Bookchin was critical of ecocentrism for not explicitly recognising the importance of societal hierarchies in exacerbating human domination of nature.

Decentralisation In ecological terms, this refers to societies that are based on small settlements such as communes, villages or bioregions that achieve sustainability through a high level of self-sufficiency, making them less dependent on (and exploitative of) their natural environment.

Society

REVISED

- Ecologists are critical of society's obsession with **consumerism**, arguing that it threatens sustainability and that it is not a true form of human consciousness.
- Ecologists argue for a shift to a new environmental consciousness of post-materialism. From here new environmental ethics would decrease consumerism and increase sustainability.

Consumerism A psychological and cultural belief system focusing on the consumption of goods and services to achieve individual fulfilment and drive economic growth.

> **Mechanistic world view** In the post-Enlightenment era, the dominant view in science is that nature is like a machine where parts can be repaired or replaced in isolation from each other. It is the opposite of holism, in which nature is perceived as being interconnected like a single organism.

- Deep green ecologists argue for societal change from industrialism to small-scale, self-sufficient communities where the **mechanistic world view** would be replaced by a holistic world view.
- Shallow green ecologists argue that society must realign its attitude to the natural world so that it is protecting rather than exploiting the environment.
- Social ecologists argue that environmental protection must be preceded by a societal transformation. Eco-anarchism and ecosocialism both require communist economic systems to replace traditional capitalism, while ecofeminists require the overthrow of patriarchy.

The economy

- Ecologism is divided on its attitude towards the economy. Deep green ecologists argue that capitalism, which underpins the modern economy, must be abolished if the environment is to survive. Shallow green ecologists argue that ecologism can co-exist with capitalism.
- Deep green ecologists argue that capitalism's insatiable desire for growth is inconsistent with ecologism due to capitalism's relentless consumption of natural resources.
- Deep green ecologists argue that the mechanistic view of the world, which dominates modern economics, means that society does not fully understand the holistic nature of the environment or the damage that capitalism causes to the planet.
- Deep green ecologists and social ecologists such as eco-anarchists and ecosocialists argue that capitalism must be destroyed via revolution to ensure environmental protection. The economy will continue via a communist model. Private property reinforces anthropocentrism and must be replaced by collective ownership so that land has ecocentric benefits.
- Shallow green ecologists argue that the state can regulate so that economic growth and ecologism can co-exist. This would involve carbon taxes, developing sustainable energy and global agreements such as the Paris accord.
- Some shallow green ecologists argue that capitalism will adapt to a consumer choice model. This green capitalism will see consumers demand environmentally sound products, which capitalism will supply, resulting in increased sustainability.

Now test yourself

TESTED

1 Identify three ecological ideas about the following themes (one idea should be deep green, one should be shallow green, one should be social ecology).
   (a) Human nature.
   (b) The state.
   (c) Society.
   (d) The economy.

Answers on p. 111

Different types of ecologism

Deep green

Deep green ecologists argue that human consciousness is anthropocentric, which has had a devastating effect on ecological sustainability. Human consciousness must undergo a revolutionary change, embracing ecocentrism and strong sustainability. To achieve this, humans must develop a new environmental consciousness embracing holism, which will lead to radical environmental ethics that will underpin the organisation of the state, society and the economy.

Some key ideas of deep green ecologists include the following:

- **Holism** is a core idea of deep green ecologism which perceives the world as an interconnected single organic whole.
- Holism is a reaction against the rationalistic mechanistic world view dominant since the Enlightenment, whereby science perceives nature as separate explainable component parts which exist for human benefit.
- The mechanistic world view argues that humans are rational enough to understand the consequences of the damage done to the natural world and intelligent enough to remedy it.
- Holism refutes these beliefs. The natural world is organic, not a machine of component parts, so the analogy is flawed. When human actions harm one part of nature, this will affect other parts, an outcome which cannot be readily predicted or even understood.
- The interconnectedness of the ecosystem is incredibly complex and beyond our complete understanding. So humans must be cautious about tampering with nature, as the effects can be extremely unpredictable and irreversible. This is vital to ensure sustainability.
- For holism to succeed, humans must embrace an environmental consciousness that overcomes the dominant anthropocentric world view. This will involve a deep identification with the non-human world and a belief that a radical change in human nature is needed to transform society.
- An environmental consciousness based on holism will lead to radical environmental ethics. Environmental ethics argue that everything within the biosphere has an intrinsic value. Aldo Leopold's land ethic included 'soil, waters, plants and animals'.
- Deep green ecologists are critical of pressure groups and political parties for focusing on single issues such as fracking or animal rights as opposed to promoting a radical holistic environmental consciousness.
- Biocentrism places nature rather than humans at the centre of the world view. Deep green ecologists argue for biocentric diversity and ecocentrism.
- Modern economies are built upon industrialism's belief in unlimited growth based on the provably false assumption that resources are infinite.
- Strong sustainability is the most extreme form of sustainability and opposes economic growth and the obsession with materialism and consumerism.
- Economic activity must be built around preserving natural capital. E.F. Schumacher's model of small-scale communities is an example of strong sustainability.
- Reforming modern economies (weak sustainability), as advocated by shallow green ecologists, is pointless because industrialism and

Holism Theories of nature and ecology that stress the idea that the whole of the earth is a single organism and that ecological problems should not be treated separately, but as part of a 'whole earth' solution. It stands in opposition to mechanistic theories.

Revision activity

Revise the following deep green ecologist principles:
- environmental ethics
- environmental consciousness
- post-materialism
- anti-consumerism.

Exam practice answers and quick quizzes at
www.hoddereducation.co.uk/myrevisionnotesdownloads

capitalism are too entrenched. President Trump's withdrawal of the USA from the Paris accord in 2017 was a prime example of why a new radical environmental consciousness with radical environmental ethics is essential.

- Post-Enlightenment rationalism, coupled with humankind's need to dominate nature due to capitalism and consumerism, is too embedded in the human psyche to be reformed. State and society need to be radically transformed.

- The reformist ideas of shallow green ecologists are not radical enough because they do not change human consciousness, which remains anthropocentric. Humans are not masters or stewards of nature and enlightened anthropocentrism is a contradiction in terms.

Key thinker

E.F. Schumacher (1911–77)

Ernst Friedrich Schumacher influenced ecological thinking by attacking traditional economics and providing a decentralised model of environmental ethics.

The main ideas of E.F. Schumacher were as follows:

- Traditional economics was based on false premises:
  - Obsession with GDP growth fuels a harmful human consciousness where consumerism and materialism are incorrectly correlated to happiness.
  - Humans treat natural resources as if they were infinite and this recklessness destroys local environments and is ultimately unsustainable.
- The solutions are threefold: limit the insatiable desire for economic growth, revert to simpler technologies so less of the earth's resources are

eroded, and replace traditional economics with Buddhist economics.

- Buddhist economics is based on a simpler economic structure, on wellbeing rather than consumption, where humans are content to appreciate what Schumacher called 'enoughness'.
- It advocates small, self-sufficient communities and small-scale organisations, using local resources, with an economy based on strong sustainability.
- This was a reaction against globalised corporations and industrialised cities. Schumacher's Buddhist economics argued for pastoralism: a return to a simpler form of existence where humans lived in smaller communities and enjoyed a more natural relationship with rural life.
- The Buddhist spiritual aspect to pastoralism was that a simpler kind of existence would lead to a higher form of environmental consciousness.

Deep green solutions

Deep green ecologism is coherent in that it wants to radically transform society by altering human consciousness from anthropocentric to ecocentric. However, there is no consensus about what a deep green society would look like or how it would function:

- E.F. Schumacher argued for pastoralism, a return to a simpler existence and to smaller communities. This would involve strong sustainability and localism, with a focus on quality of life and humans reconnecting with nature, divorcing themselves from both traditional economics and the obsession with materialism/consumerism.
- Schumacher argued for **Buddhist economics** where the focus is on people, not profit, and where wellbeing is maximised by living in balance with nature in small communities that aspire for 'enoughness' through minimising and not maximising consumption.

> **Buddhist economics**
> An idea associated with E.F. Schumacher which argues that people should find simpler ways of living and working with limited desires for goods and a more natural spiritual relationship with the environment.

- Murray Bookchin argued for 'ecotopia', a society based on an anarcho-communistic model. This would involve abolishing private property and redistributing wealth on a needs basis. Environmental consciousness and environmental ethics would change as humans wish to live in harmony with nature rather than to dominate it.
- Paul Ehrlich argued for population control as it threatens the biosphere.
- Peter Berg challenged nation-state borders, proposing a series of local communities, dubbed 'bioregions', whose boundaries were created by environmental features. This would create a new environmental ethics of 'living democracy' where decision making would be taken locally and focused on strong sustainability.

> **Revision activity**
>
> What are the following key thinkers' attitudes towards the economy?
> - E.F. Schumacher
> - Murray Bookchin.

Shallow green

REVISED

Shallow green ecologists, unlike deep greens, do not require humans to undergo a dramatic shift in environmental consciousness. Reformist in nature, their ideas cluster around enlightened anthropocentrism and weak sustainability.

- Enlightened anthropocentrism is the belief that humans can live in harmony with nature through reforming existing political and economic structures so that they act as a 'steward' of nature.
- Sustainability: modern economies are built upon the industrialism belief in unlimited growth based on the false assumption that resources are infinite. The green movement responded with the concept of sustainability to maintain the health of the ecological system by applying **limits to growth**. Sustainability includes biodiversity, preserving natural resources, preserving nature and controlling atmospheric and water pollution.

> **Limits to growth** The planet has finite resources, which places physical limits on industrial growth.

Weak sustainability is far less radical than deep green's strong sustainability. It argues for:

- managerialism: the belief that the state at the national and international level can regulate environmental problems
- global action: international conferences and agreements such as the 1985 Helsinki Agreement on controlling harmful emissions, the 1997 Kyoto Agreement to prevent climate change, and the 2015 Paris accord where 196 states committed to halt the rise in global warming; the UK's Climate Change Act 2008 promised an 80% reduction in emissions by 2050
- governments to tax air emissions using financial disincentives to encourage industry to become more sustainable
- sustainable energy: using positive incentives such as tax breaks and government investment to utilise wind, wave, thermal and nuclear power, none of which uses up finite resources
- biodiversity: to protect flora and fauna under threat of extinction
- local waste recycling schemes
- preservation of the countryside through strict planning controls
- energy conservation via better insulation of new buildings.

> **Typical mistake**
>
> Students often discuss sustainability without differentiating between strong and weak sustainability.

In green capitalism there is an emphasis on how environmental problems can be tackled through market-based solutions:
- Pressure from ethical consumers can incentivise sustainable capitalism, e.g. Nestlé's announcement that its palm olive supply chain will have a zero-deforestation policy.

- Finite resources such as oil and coal will increase in price and the result will be a reduction in their use.
- Media campaigns for consumers will focus on energy-saving measures.

Shallow green ecologism is coherent in its ideas, although there remains debate over which is the most effective form of enlightened anthropocentrism: managerialism or green economy.

Social ecology

REVISED

Coined by Murray Bookchin, this is a collective term for traditions that require a revolutionary social change within their specific area before environmental changes can occur. The three areas of social ecology are as follows.

Ecosocialism

- Ecosocialists argue that capitalism is the cause of environmental problems and only a revolution can solve this issue.
- Capitalism's desire for exponential growth and profit is relentless and comes at the expense of the environment.
- Capitalism commoditises nature so that natural resources are reduced to an economic value rather than their own intrinsic worth.
- Ecosocialist John Bellamy Foster's reinterpretation of Marxist writings led him to conclude that there will be a 'metabolic rift' between nature and capitalist production. There will be revolution, ecosocialist in nature, as workers rebel against a shortage of resources such as food, water and energy.
- Green capitalism is flawed, as capitalism's core values are profit and continual growth and not ecological concerns. Profit will always supersede environmental concern. President Trump withdrawing the USA from the Paris accord in 2017 is an example of this.
- Private property underpins the idea that people can dominate nature by owning land — ecosocialists advocate collective ownership.

Eco-anarchism

- Eco-anarchism, associated with Murray Bookchin, argues that people's desire to dominate has been translated into their disastrous treatment of nature.
- Eco-anarchists argue that the need to dominate is inherent in capitalism and is reinforced by the authoritarian, hierarchical structures of the state.
- Both the state and capitalism must be overthrown and human consciousness will then shift from one of domination to one of harmony, both in human relations and with the environment, creating a new environmental consciousness.
- An eco-anarchist society would create new environmental ethics, of decentralisation, with small communities or bioregions forming a symbiotic relationship with the natural environment.

Exam tip

Do not fall into the trap of equating communist governments with being ecosocialist. China and the USSR both had poor records environmentally. However, one can argue that neither was genuinely socialist and that in its pure form socialism, divorced from capitalism's environmentally destructive consciousness, could deliver ecological responsibility.

Typical mistake

Deep green and social ecology are far removed from most students' experiences and sometimes answers can be cynical or dismissive of such ideas. Remember, the examiner wants to see an understanding of the rationale behind these ideas. Students giving one-sided anthropocentric arguments will lose lots of marks for not giving due attention to ecocentrism.

- These decentralised communities would practise strong sustainability. Individuals would be directly involved with the environment, unlike capitalist consumers who are detached from nature.

Ecofeminism

- Men dominate and oppress women through patriarchy and nature through capitalism and post-Enlightenment science.
- Ecofeminists such as Carolyn Merchant argue that women have a far more caring attitude towards the environment than men do.
- If patriarchy is overthrown, humans can share a new environmental consciousness based on an egalitarian relationship between men and women.
- This new equal status between genders will create new environmental ethics, with humans treating the environment as an equal, which will encourage co-existence and end humankind's domination over nature.

> **Revision activity**
>
> How do the following perceive and understand ecology?
> - Dark green.
> - Shallow green.
> - Eco-anarchism.
> - Ecosocialism.
> - Ecofeminism.

Key thinker

Carolyn Merchant (1936–)

Merchant is a pioneer of ecofeminism and was one of the first to see a correlation between man's domination of women and the domination of nature.

The main ideas of Carolyn Merchant are as follows:
- She is opposed to the mechanistic male view of science and nature.
- Merchant blames the Enlightenment ideas of Francis Bacon, René Descartes and Isaac Newton for altering human consciousness. Pre-Enlightenment humans believed in co-existence with nature; post-Enlightenment (and rational individualism) humans began to believe that they could explain and dominate the natural world.
- The ideas of the Enlightenment led to a belief that science is superior to nature. Bacon argued that nature should be subservient to the needs of humanity.
- These ideas led to a remodelling of human consciousness where science was perceived as superior to nature and subservient to the domination of humans, which, when coupled to the demands of capitalism, has led to ecological devastation.

- Merchant uses the metaphor that nature is female and that nature's 'womb' has yielded to the intrusive 'forceps' of science.
- Merchant famously equates this triumph of science over nature as like a death. Her key work, *The Death of Nature* (1980), reminds us of this idea.
- The oppression and death of nature are linked to gender oppression.
- Merchant links the domination of nature with patriarchy, man's wish to dominate women.
- Nature's resources are exploited to facilitate capitalism in a male-dominated world.
- Nature is oppressed as its resources are plundered, and women are trapped by patriarchy and forced to breed the next generation of workers.
- Merchant argued that patriarchy must be overthrown and a new egalitarian relationship between men and women would emerge, creating a new environmental consciousness.
- This 'partnership ethic' would create new environmental ethics and a sustainable partnership with nature, once 'a social reconstruction', i.e. a change in human consciousness, had occurred.

> **Exam tip**
>
> Merchant's ideas are influenced by socialist key thinker Friedrich Engels (see page 51), who argued that capitalism confined women's role to the private sphere of domestic life, where their principal task was to bear children and unwittingly socialise them into the next generation of workers.

It is common for examiners to question how broadly the term 'ecology' has been employed, which will require you to demonstrate that you understand the various branches and their differences. You must use examples from the key thinkers to corroborate your points.

Typical mistake

Do not argue that ecologism is the only political idea that promotes protecting the environment. Conservative, liberal and socialist governments have promoted environmentally friendly policies all over the world, such as national parks and animal welfare.

Now test yourself

TESTED

2 Define holism.
3 Why do followers of holism disagree with the mechanistic world view?
4 Define anthropocentrism.
5 Define ecocentrism.
6 Why do ecologists object to:
  (a) industrialism
  (b) consumerism?
7 Describe the two types of sustainability.
8 Identify two ideas that unite all ecologists and then two that divide them.

Answers on pp. 111–12

Exam practice

You must use appropriate thinkers you have studied to support your answer and consider both sides in a balanced way.
1 To what extent do the different strands of ecologism agree about human nature? [24]
2 To what extent do the different strands of ecologism agree on the role of the state? [24]
3 To what extent is ecologism incompatible with the modern industrial economy? [24]

Answers and quick quiz 8 online

ONLINE

Summary

You should now have an understanding of:
- the great divide within ecology ideas, which concerns deep green ecologists arguing for ecocentrism and shallow green ecologists arguing for enlightened anthropocentrism
- holism, the idea that the planet can be understood only as an interrelated whole, which is the one unifying theme of the different branches of ecologism
- how ecology can be revolutionary (deep green, social ecology), reformist (shallow ecology) but also right wing (green capitalism) and left wing (ecosocialism) — this makes ecology the most diverse political idea that you will study
- how deep green ecology is unique in utterly rejecting the primacy of human interests
- the contribution to the development of liberal thought of at least the five key thinkers.

Chapter 1

1 (a) – Humankind is rational.
   – People are enlightened or capable of enlightenment.
   – People prefer to take actions with good ends rather than bad ends.
   – Some liberals say people are self-seeking.
   – People are competitive but also sensitive to the needs of others.
  (b) – A liberal society will be tolerant.
   – A liberal society will respect individual liberties.
   – A liberal society will defend human rights.
  (c) – A liberal economy is likely to be based on free markets.
   – Liberals generally support capitalism.
   – There should be a degree of social justice.
  (d) – The liberal state should be based on the rule of law.
   – There should be a democratic system and government by consent.
   – There should be a firm constitution which limits the power of government.

2

Liberal idea	Type of liberalism
Negative liberty represents an absence of restraint and it is the highest value for liberals.	Classical liberalism
People have a moral obligation to care for the welfare of others and positive liberty is as important as negative liberty.	New liberalism
Social evils and deprivation are as important curtailments of freedom as laws and over-powerful government.	Welfare liberalism
All sections of society are worthy of equal respect and should be tolerated.	Classical liberalism
Equality of opportunity can help to ensure that all people in society can achieve self-realisation.	New liberalism
Constitutional reform is essential if government is to be controlled and equal rights are to be guaranteed.	Contemporary liberalism

3 (a) Classical liberals support a minimal, very limited state while modern liberals believe the state can be expanded in order to create equality of opportunity, welfare and social justice.
  (b) Classical liberals are suspicious of welfare as it takes away the individual's drive to improve themselves. Modern liberals accept the need for state-led welfare as it creates social justice and prevents undeserved deprivation.
  (c) Classical liberals are supporters of free-market capitalism whereas modern liberals accept that capitalism should be modified and regulated to prevent excessive inequality and deprivation.

4

Liberal idea	Example of a key thinker
Inequality can be justified if it does not result in the worst off in society becoming even more deprived.	John Rawls
The state is the result of a social contract between government and the people.	John Locke
Representative democracy is superior to popular democracy.	J.S. Mill
All members of society should have the same opportunities, including women.	Betty Friedan
The state is justified in creating laws only if they are designed to prevent some people doing harm to others through their actions.	J.S. Mill
Welfare supplied by the state can be justified if it guarantees distributive justice.	John Rawls

5 Negative liberty is 'freedom from' and means the absence of restrictions on our actions, while positive freedom means 'freedom to' and means the existence of conditions which allow us to achieve self-realisation, such as equality of opportunity and welfare.

6 (a) Because they propose a return to a form of economy which existed in the past, i.e. a free-market economy with no state interference.
  (b) Because they wish to strengthen controls on government, improve democratic

Exam practice answers and quick quizzes at
www.hoddereducation.co.uk/myrevisionnotesdownloads

accountability, reinforce the protection of rights and introduce a fairer electoral system.

(c) Because she insisted on equal rights for women and wished to widen opportunities for women. (d) Positive liberty promotes opportunities for individuals to achieve self-realisation while negative liberty refers to the absence of restrictions on our actions.

(e) His 1942 report led to the foundation of the welfare state in the 1940s and introduced the idea of 'welfare liberalism' with an expanded state.

(f) He saw it as the 'tyranny of the majority' which would oppress minority interests.

7 (a) Positive freedom (or liberty).

(b) Minimal state.

(c) Neo-liberalism.

(d) Equality of opportunity.

(e) Formal equality.

(f) Social contract.

(g) Meritocracy.

8 In order to create greater equality the state needs to intervene in society in various ways which may restrict individual liberty. For example, it may involve high taxes, regulation of industry and a compulsory system of welfare.

Chapter 2

1 Traditional conservatives argue that a society cannot be created or contrived but rather emerges organically like a living organism. Organic society is hierarchical and the ruling elite has duties and social obligations to maintain society's wellbeing. In practice, an organic society consists of numerous interlocking local communities.

2 Traditional conservatives, one-nation conservatives and Christian democrats are distrustful of rationalism as they believe humans to be intellectually imperfect. Therefore, they argue, humans should be guided by pragmatism, which is informed by tradition and empiricism. Neo-liberals have a positive view of human nature and therefore prefer rationalism and principle (rather than pragmatism) to guide their actions.

3 Neo-liberals favour an atomistic society that values individual freedom and autonomy. They argue that individual freedom is restricted by the duties and social obligations that are inherent in an organic society.

4 (a) Ayn Rand.

(b) Michael Oakeshott.

(c) Thomas Hobbes.

(d) Robert Nozick.

(e) Edmund Burke.

5 (a) The organic view perceives society as being like a living organism with unequal but interdependent parts. Atomism perceives society as a collection of self-interested and self-sufficient individuals.

(b) Rand is not an anarchist because she requires a small state to maintain free markets and social laissez-faire and to defend borders.

(c) Conservatism, apart from the neo-liberal branch of the New Right, views humans as intellectually imperfect and incapable of the infallible theories promised by rationalism.

(d) Nozick offered neo-liberal arguments for the role of the state being limited:
   – A miniaturist government with minimal interference in the lives of individuals makes for the best society.
   – The state's primary function is to protect individual human rights via negative freedom.

(e) They argue that the state must change to conserve society, usually by sanctioning social and economic reform to reduce societal disorder.

6 (a) Most branches of conservatism argue that humans are intellectually, morally and psychologically imperfect. Neo-liberals are more positive about human nature. Unlike the rest of conservatism, they argue humans are capable of rationalism.

(b) Most branches of conservatism view society as organic. Neo-liberals view society as atomistic.

(c) Most branches of conservatism argue that the state must intervene to maintain the organic society. Neo-liberals argue for a minimum state that protects negative freedom and protects against foreign invasion.

(d) All conservatives support the free market but most agree on intervention, to differing degrees, to ensure the health of the organic society, e.g. the welfare state. Neo-liberals believe in laissez-faire, free-market economics with no welfare state and minimal taxation.

7 Most conservatives argue that the state must intervene at times to preserve the organic society, changing to conserve. Neo-liberals believe in an atomistic society and therefore require a miniaturist state.

8 Supranationalism is when states pool sovereignty and act collectively, as with the EU. Most conservatives prefer nation-states retaining sovereignty and cooperating rather than integrating. Neo-liberals prefer miniaturist

states and therefore distrust federal structures like the EU.

9 Due to human imperfection, without the state humans would live in 'a state of war'. The social compact involves surrendering individual freedoms to the state and the state ensuring the safety of individuals via the structures of society.

10 The English had failed in their responsibilities in governing America. The revolution only removed the English — its society remained, informed by empiricism and traditions. The French were also failed by ineffective rulers, but their revolution discarded empiricism and tradition for utopian idealism, 'philosophical abstractions', which meant the French state disastrously descended into violence and chaos.

11 Oakeshott believes in human imperfection and has a lack of faith in human ability to understand reality or create principles and theories. He therefore distrusts rationalism, arguing that we should be sceptical of such doctrinaire thinking and that any changes to society should be cautiously informed by pragmatism and empiricism.

12 She meant an atomistic society; individual comprehension of reality, which will lead to self-realisation and self-fulfilment; a belief in individuals' capacity for rationalism.

13 (a) Anti-permissiveness.

(b) Human imperfection.

(c) Laissez-faire.

(d) Noblesse oblige.

(e) Atomism.

(f) Radical.

(g) Authority.

(h) Hierarchy.

(i) Change to conserve.

(j) Empiricism.

Chapter 3

1 (a) Individuals possess a common humanity and are essentially rational social creatures who naturally gravitate towards cooperation and sociability. Human nature is not fixed but is easily shaped by an individual's environment, so human nature and human behaviour are socially determined by society.

(b) Human nature and society are closely interlinked, as individuals are products of their society. Consequently, if society is to be improved, there will have to be a corresponding improvement in the behaviour of individuals. Social democrats argue that society will benefit through equality of welfare to tackle poverty.

(c) Revolutionary socialists argue that the state will no longer be needed after the revolution as society will be free of internal contradictions and class conflict. All other aspects of socialism require state intervention to differing degrees to facilitate their version of socialism.

(d) Revolutionary socialists want capitalism abolished and replaced with an economy based on collective ownership of property and the workers controlling the means of production. Social democrats and the Third Way think the worst aspects of capitalism can be reformed. Social democrats argue for state-managed intervention, while the Third Way argues for co-opting the efficiency of the free market to deliver increased equality of opportunity.

2 Exploitation occurs inevitability to maximise profits of owners who deprive their workers of their surplus value. Capitalism's need to expand is insatiable and it will seek out new markets to dominate.

3 Materialist theory claims that economic and class factors explain historical and social development. History is a dialectic class struggle where the ruling class dominates and exploits everyone else. The economic system (slavery, feudalism, capitalism) influences all other aspects of society.

4 This meant a transitional phase where the state would control the means of production and distribution.

5 Communism was a society free of internal contradictions, private property and class conflict that hitherto had been present in historical development, as society had finally reached an end point with a unified communist consciousness. History was a process of class struggle, so the arrival of a communist society meant the end of history.

6 Luxemburg disagreed with Marx and Engel's historical materialism, which stated that capitalism must reach a final stage before it can be abolished. She theorised that communism could happen in less economically developed societies.

7 – Cooperative communities of utopian socialists.
– Collective ownership of revolutionary socialists as espoused by Marx and Engels and Luxemburg.
– State-managed capitalism and nationalisation as espoused by social democracy and key thinker Anthony Crosland.

8 Marx and Engels and Luxemburg thought capitalism too powerful and inherently selfish to be reformed — it had to be eradicated via revolution.

9 Social class underpins three crucial elements of their theory: historical materialism, dialectical

change and the development of revolutionary consciousness.

10 Luxemburg realised the dangers of tyranny if the members of a society (even after a revolution) did not have the vote or freedom of speech. She was sceptical of Marx and Engels' theory of historical materialism and their claim that society could be free of the internal contradictions that would be necessary for democracy to be obsolete.

11 Webb thought that only a skilled elite could deliver a socialist society and she had little faith in the workers being able to organise this themselves. It would therefore require central state planning of production, distribution and exchange to achieve a true socialist society. It was a top-down view of a socialist state that would replace capitalism.

12 Crosland argued that the state must manage capitalism, reforming its negative aspects so that it benefits the many and not the few. This would involve a mixed economy and the state pursuing Keynesian economic policy, which would ensure full employment, low inflation and economic growth. The proceeds of capitalism would be shared via social justice, which would redistribute wealth via the welfare system.

13 Giddens argued that attempts to manage capitalism were inefficient and ineffective, claiming that the economy thrived under free-market, laissez-faire policies and not Keynesian intervention. Likewise, the redistribution of wealth via social democracy's welfare state had created a dependency culture. The state should instead increase equalities of opportunity to decrease inequalities of outcome and offset the negative effects of the free market.

Chapter 4

1 Most feminists are equality feminists, arguing that the physical biological differences of sex play no role in defining innate gender characteristics. Rather, it is the patriarchal nature of society that influences gender traits. This cultural explanation has been the basis for radical and liberal feminism seeking to change society. Post-modern feminists have argued for intersectionality, which challenges the idea that gender is the singular most important factor. Difference feminists have challenged the idea that gender is a cultural phenomenon, arguing that biological sexual differences define innate gender characteristics.

2 Liberal feminists believe that society can be reformed so that patriarchy is eliminated. Socialist feminists argue that economics as well as gender determine female oppression. Socialist

feminists have differed in their solutions, arguing that society should be reformed or revolutionised to tackle these intertwining factors.

3 'The personal is political' is the idea that patriarchy must be understood not just in the public sphere of society, as liberal feminists would have it, but also within private family life that had hitherto been largely ignored. Radical feminists, highlighting the importance of family life for socialising patriarchal behaviour, transformed this personal private sphere of life into a political concern.

4 Equality feminists argue that biological sexual differences are irrelevant in determining gender characteristics. Gender characteristics are determined by the patriarchal nature of society. Difference feminists argue that gender characteristics are determined by biological sexual differences and that men and women have distinct and natural gender traits.

5 Liberal feminism is primarily concerned with reforming the public sphere of society by eradicating sexual discrimination so that men and women are treated equally. Radical feminism is concerned with both the public sphere of society and the private sphere of the family in its analysis of patriarchy. Radical feminists reject reform and prefer revolution to transform society. Radical feminism is not coherent in its solutions as it proposes a number of conflicting revolutionary societies.

6 Radical feminism argues that patriarchal gender oppression is the main factor in determining a woman's fate, whereas socialist feminism argues that women are also oppressed economically, primarily by capitalism.

7 Post-feminism argues that most of the battles of inequality have been won and that women need to move on. Post-modern feminism disagrees and argues for intersectionality, which challenges the notion that gender is the singular factor for determining female oppression. Post-modern feminism would strongly disagree with the post-feminist postulation that women have won most battles of inequality, arguing that post-feminism articulates only the narrow view of middle-class women in western society.

8 Post-modern feminism argues that other branches of feminism do not embrace the complexity of reality and that existence is too complicated for a woman's fate to be determined by only one factor: gender. Likewise, the very construct of a woman is simplistic as women are more than just their gender — class, race, age and religion all play a part in forming identity. This is why post-modern feminists support intersectionality, which embraces the complexity of women, who have multiple, overlapping identities.

9 (a) Legal equality.

(b) Difference feminism.

(c) Intersectionality.

(d) Patriarchy.

(e) Equality feminism.

(f) Discrimination.

(g) Gender stereotypes.

(h) Reserve army of labour.

(i) Reformist.

(j) Public sphere.

(k) Otherness.

(l) Equality of opportunity.

(m) Essentialism.

(n) Political equality.

(o) Cultural feminism.

(p) Private sphere.

(q) Gender equality.

10 (a) Sheila Rowbotham.

(b) Charlotte Perkins Gilman.

(c) Simone de Beauvoir.

(d) Kate Millett.

(e) bell hooks.

Chapter 5

1 (a) Private judgement.

(b) Mutual aid.

(c) Federalism.

(d) Egoism.

2 Bakunin insisted the state must be smashed through violent revolution. Marx agreed but insisted that the capitalist state should be replaced (temporarily) by a new workers' state — the dictatorship of the proletariat. Bakunin argued that this simply exchanged one form of oppression for another.

3 (a) Kropotkin had a very optimistic view of human nature, believing people are naturally sociable and wish to live in voluntary communities. He also believed we prefer equality to inequality.

(b) Thoreau believed mankind resents over-regulation and prefers absolute liberty. He also believed we can achieve self-realisation by becoming self-sufficient and not relying on others.

(c) Goldman believed that if the state was removed, the natural mutual love between people would take over to create a harmonious society. She also insisted on equality between men and women.

(d) Similar to Kropotkin, Bakunin was optimistic that people can live in natural communities and cooperate voluntarily with each other. He believed the most natural communities would be based on occupational groups.

4 (a) The need to abolish the state, that all individuals are sovereign, anti-clericalism.

(b) Whether humans is essentially driven by sociability or egoism, whether we prefer to live a solitary existence or in social groups, whether all private property should be abolished.

5 Possible answers are:
   - Free-market capitalism and economic competition are natural and desirable.
   - The state should not regulate industry and markets.
   - There should be little or no public welfare.
   - Trade unions should be suppressed.
   - Monopolies should be broken up.

Chapter 6

1 (a) Chauvinism.

(b) Patriotism.

(c) Racialism.

(d) Volksgeist.

(e) Pan-nationalism.

2 A state is a political reality, ruled over by a government that is recognised by other states. States may be made up of one nation or a number of national groups. A nation is the collective state of mind of a people who believe they have a common circumstance of birth. Nations may exist without a state or a national group may form only part of a state. Where the nation and state come together, it can be described as a nation-state.

3 (a) Marcus Garvey.

(b) Rousseau or Mazzini.

(c) Marcus Garvey or Fidel Castro.

(d) Charles Maurras.

4 Radical nationalism refers to extreme forms of right-wing nationalism. It is also associated with the synthesis between racism and nationalism. Radical nationalists see the interests of the nation as having the highest social value and believe this should be pursued at all costs. German Nazism was a classic example.

5 (a) Republican nationalism.

(b) Cultural nationalism.

(c) Anti-colonial nationalism.

(d) Radical nationalism.

6 (a) – Progressive nationalists hope to see the improvement of a society while regressive nationalists wish to return to a former age.
   - Progressive nationalists see nationalism in terms of personal, individual development

of people while regressive nationalists tend to see the interests of the nation and those of individuals as identical.

- – Progressive nationalists tend to be liberal or socialist, with a clear view of future development, while regressive nationalists stress solidarity rather than progress.

(b) – Liberal nationalists are also democrats while conservatives place the solidarity of the nation above democracy.
- – Liberal nationalists see individual and collective national liberty as part of the same movement while conservative nationalists place national interests above individual interests.
- – Liberal nationalists see strong nationalism as a vehicle for enhancing liberty while conservative nationalists stress unity and cohesion.

(c) – Racism is based on irrational attitudes to race while racialism tends to be scientific.
- – Racists see one race as superior to others while racialists are more concerned with racial differences than a hierarchy of races.
- – Racialism is value neutral while racism places some values above others.

Chapter 7

1 (a) Universalism.
   (b) Assimilation.
   (c) Differential rights.
   (d) Segregation.
2 (a) Deep diversity.
   (b) Shallow diversity.
   (c) Shallow diversity.
   (d) Deep diversity.
3 (a) Cosmopolitan integration.
   (b) Universalism.
   (c) Equality of opportunity.
   (d) Culture.
4 (a) Isaiah Berlin.
   (b) Tariq Modood.
   (c) Charles Taylor.
   (d) Bhikhu Parekh.

Chapter 8

1 (a) Deep green idea: environmental consciousness must be transformed, abandoning anthropocentrism for ecocentrism.

Shallow green idea: environmental consciousness must alter and become one of enlightened anthropocentrism. This will see

the human race act as a responsible steward for the environment.

Social ecology idea: a radical social change is needed before environmental consciousness is possible. For example, ecofeminists require the overthrow of patriarchy.

(b) Deep green idea: has a negative view of the state, arguing for its power to be reduced by decentralisation or abolished completely.

Shallow green idea: argues for managerialism, where the state intervenes at the national and the international level to regulate environmental problems.

Social ecology idea: ecosocialists view the state as enforcing capitalism and industrialism. It will therefore need to be abolished so that society can be communist in nature.

(c) Deep green idea: argues for societal change, from industrialism to small-scale, self-sufficient communities, ensuring strong sustainability.

Shallow green idea: argues that society must realign its attitude to the natural world so that it is protecting rather than exploiting, ensuring weak sustainability.

Social ecology idea: argues that environmental protection must be preceded by a societal transformation. Eco-anarchism requires a communist society to ensure strong sustainability in a stateless society.

(d) Deep green idea: capitalism must be destroyed to ensure environmental protection. The economy will continue via a communist model.

Shallow green idea: argues that the state can regulate so that economic growth and ecologism can co-exist.

Social ecology idea: ecosocialism and eco-anarchism both argue that capitalism must be destroyed via revolution to ensure environmental protection. The economy will continue via a communist model.

2 Holism perceives the world as an interconnected single organic whole and is a reaction against the rationalistic mechanistic world view.

3 Holism disagrees with the rationalist scientific premise that nature can be divided into explainable component parts that can be understood, fixed or replaced in isolation. Holism believes the opposite: that everything within nature is interrelated, much of it beyond human comprehension.

4 Anthropocentrism is the idea that human interests are of primary importance, with an intrinsic value, and the rest of nature is a resource to be exploited for the benefit of the

human race. Shallow green ecologists argue for 'enlightened anthropocentrism' whereby humans act as stewards of the environment, protecting the natural world so that it can continue to support human life.

5 Ecocentrism is a nature-centred rather than a human-centred system of values. It therefore gives priority to ecological balance over human wants and needs.

6 (a) Industrialism's insatiable utilisation of science and technology to achieve mass limitless economic growth, via mass production, is in conflict with the sustainability of the ecological system. Ecologists argue that there must be limits to growth due to the finite earth and finite natural resources.

  (b) Consumerism creates false needs and a false human consciousness, as the consumption of material goods is damaging to the environment and ultimately does not bring genuine happiness. Ecologists argue that an environmental consciousness built on environmental ethics will bring true happiness.

7 Deep green ecologists argue for strong sustainability, which would radically alter human activity by opposing economic growth and materialism, enabling society to shift to self-contained, small communities. Shallow green ecologists argue for weak sustainability, which is reformist and proposes more environmentally sound capitalism.

8 Two ideas that unite all ecologists:
  – The non-human world deserves and demands central consideration within the organisation of state (nationally and internationally), society and economy.
  – Sustainability, the ability of the ecological system (the planet) to maintain its health over time, is essential.

Two ideas that divide all ecologists:
  – Deep green ecologists argue for strong sustainability while shallow green ecologists argue for weak sustainability.
  – Shallow green ecologists are anthropocentric and argue that society can be reformed so environmental problems are successfully managed via green capitalism, managerialism and technological solutions. Deep green ecologists are ecocentric and think that society needs a far more radical change of consciousness and must embrace ecocentrism and biocentric equality.